THE DEVIL'S
CONCUBINE

THE DEVIL'S CONCUBINE
FROM JEZEBEL TO JESUS

Dawn Michelle

The stories in this book reflect the author's recollection of events. Some names, locations, and identifying characteristics have been changed to protect the privacy of those depicted. Dialogue has been recreated from memory.

The Devil's Concubine
From Jezebel to Jesus
Dawn Michelle

Printed in the United States of America

First printing: July 2021

ISBN: 978-1-7339545-5-6

Heavenly Father, may the words of this book reach and save the multitude in the name of Jesus. Amen.

Then Peter said unto them, Repent, and be baptized every one of you in the name of Jesus Christ for the remission of sins, and ye shall receive the gift of the Holy Ghost.
Then they that gladly received his word were baptized; and the same day there were added *unto them* about three thousand souls.
(The Holy Bible, King James Version, Acts 2:38,41)

Table of Contents

1 GOD...2

2 JEZEBEL...4

3 REPRIEVE 6

4 HEARTBREAK..7

5 LOST 9

6 LOVE 12

7 WILLFUL SIN 14

8 THERAPY 16

9 GHOST...24

10 WAYWARD 27

11 THE LAST SUPPER 34

12 THE DEVIL'S CONCUBINE..................................38

13 DEAD BODY 50

14 HUMILITY 52

15 EYES WIDE SHUT..55

16 DEATH BED 59

17 NEW BEGINNINGS 61

18 JESUS 67

19 REBIRTH 70

20 BIBLE...74

21 ILLUMINATED BIBLE 79

22 DISCERNMENT 81

23 SPIRITUAL WARFARE..85

24 GOD'S FAVOR..86

25 THE VOICE AND HAND OF GOD 88

26 RAPTURE 90

27 CHURCH 92

28 FULL CIRCLE 104

29 HEAVEN 106

30 TRANSFORMATION 107

31 TEMPTATION **109**
32 WISDOM **110**
33 MARRIED TO THE LORD...**116**

FOREWARD

To the women too embarrassed to tell their stories: I
will tell mine for you.

1

GOD

And he said unto them, Go ye into all the world, and preach the gospel to every creature. (Mark 16:15)

I wasn't supposed to make it out alive. The stuff I did before getting saved could have landed me in jail, under the jail, and in eternal hell. How do you endure tribulations, and willful sin, and survive? God. I testify for those who do not know where to turn. Those who are too ashamed to ask for help. Those who have lost hope. Those who are depressed. Those who do not want to live anymore. Those who have no purpose. I felt all of these emotions before I accepted Jesus as my Lord and Savior. I want to be an example of hope and inspiration for others so that they too can ask for forgiveness no matter the sin, repent as I did, and be redeemed in time for an eternity in heaven. I am alive, I am Black, and I am well today because of my Lord and Savior Jesus Christ, and I hope my story helps someone find love and comfort in Him.

As a child, I used to cry about the world ending. Technically, I knew about the end of the world but did not know the official term. I understood the gravity of the Rapture physically, but not biblically. As I grew older, my paternal grandmother (Grandma) would always ask me if I wanted to get saved. I never wanted anything to do with it. I liked my secular music; I used to pose with my Michael Jackson *Thriller* album cover. I wasn't able to comprehend heaven and hell at that age. As an adult, I would always laugh at the people standing at street corners hollering that Jesus is coming and holding up signs of His return. I thought they were crazy till I got to know Him for myself. In a city so far away from His covenant, the current day Sodom and Gomorrah, also known as San Francisco, where temptations abound, everything goes, bad is good, and good is bad. With decades of sin weighing heavy on my shoulders and living in the city that embraces said sin, I understand now more than ever why the call to get saved was so strong here: this city is ground zero for damnation. His return *is* near. But before I tell you how I found Him, I will tell you how I lost myself.

2

Jezebel

Notwithstanding I have a few things against thee, because thou sufferest that woman Jezebel, which calleth herself a prophetess, to teach and to seduce my servants to commit fornication, and to eat things sacrificed unto idols.
And I gave her space to repent of her fornication; and she repented not.
Behold, I will cast her into a bed, and them that commit adultery with her into great tribulation, except they repent of their deeds.
(Revelation 2:20-22)

I am a cute and intelligent child till I hit puberty. Then I'm just intelligent. So, I don't get much attention. My family does their best to instill good values in me. My mom: say please and thank you, don't have sex with just anyone, and don't talk to strangers. My grandma: don't get pregnant out of wedlock, it will ruin your life; and stay within your budget. My favorite cousin: always have good posture and look cute. My paternal grandfather (Papa): education is important.

I grow up fast when my brother is born. My mom endures hardships, so I step in more to take care of him until he and I are temporarily separated, living with different family members. We eventually reunite and live under the same roof with my mom when I am a freshman in high school.

4

THE DEVIL'S CONCUBINE

My classmate introduces me to her cousin, who will change the trajectory of my life. I later learn that he is a drug dealer and a gangster with a horrible temper. He starts picking me up from school, but one day I take the bus home instead. He sees me walking from the bus stop with a guy he knows. He calls me later and asks me out on a date to the movies. He picks me up but takes me to his house instead. He says, "I saw you walking down the street with [Ricky]. If I ever see you with another man again, I will blow this pretty little face off your body." He proceeds to rape me at gunpoint. It is a rifle, and the barrel is pointing at my head. Except for the pretty little face part, I believe him. I think he is going to kill me that night. He drops me off at home an hour later. I wait next to the mailboxes to stall before going inside the apartment because I don't want my mom to wonder why I am home so soon and ask questions. So, I wait another 30 minutes, step inside the front door, and pretend as though nothing happened. My little brother can smell the rape on me, but I quickly dismiss it when he questions me. Behold, Jezebel.

Back at school, a girl named Lashonda threatens me with a gun.

"I have my piece, and you better have yours."

She thinks I want her boyfriend. My mom calls the school authorities, which only infuriates her more. She starts harassing me on bus rides home from school, wanting to fight me. I elude her every time. Later, that girl drops out of school and becomes confined to a wheelchair, by the bullet of someone else's piece.

3

Reprieve

Peace I leave with you, my peace I give unto you: not as the world giveth, give I unto you. Let not your heart be troubled, neither let it be afraid. (John 14:27)

I experience a temporary calm over my life; I find a reprieve in summer education. I enroll in multiple summer programs at the university, where I complete college-level math, English, critical thinking, and communication classes. It is a nice distraction from the chaos at home. I meet a nice girl, and we become lifelong friends. Then, in my junior and senior years of high school, I attend a program for college-bound students to take courses in the summer. We stay in the dorms during the week and return to our respective homes on the weekends. Each Sunday night, we gather in the TV room and watch *In Living Color* skits featuring Fire Marshal Bill, Vera, and Wanda. We also watch Ms. Swan on *Mad TV* on Thursday nights. And sometimes, we sit around in the hallways drinking Boone's Farm Strawberry Hill Wine. It is so much fun.

4

Heartbreak

The LORD is nigh unto them that are of a broken heart; and saveth such as be of a contrite spirit. (Psalms 34:18)

I graduate high school and enroll in college when my life takes another turn. I endure a few semesters before flunking out. There is a lot of family drama happening on both sides. The drama is fit for *The Jerry Springer Show*, but the criminal activity against my mom and brother is better suited for a *CSI* episode. It is so horrible that it further solidifies the division within the family, and it is all created by two perpetrators from within. To make matters worse, my maternal grandmother (Mama) and most of the family do not believe the allegations. I distance myself from them entirely after the age of 19 and have a relationship with only my mom, brother, and paternal side of the family.

Life gets worse. I get pregnant, have an abortion, get pregnant again, and have another abortion: two different men, one year apart. The first guy says, "I cannot believe you are killing my flesh and blood." The second guy takes off the condom the first time we have sex, and I get pregnant. He accuses me of cheating on him when I have only been faithful and says, "Have the abortion. You will thank me later."

Though I officially enroll in a Sex Education class in college before getting expelled due to poor grades, I am too ignorant to understand the gravity of the spiritual, physical, and mental impacts this will have on me later. If I had God in my heart, I would have given birth to those babies and welcomed them as blessings. I never conceive again. Is it because the last abortion destroyed my uterus? I will never know. My mom does what she can to convince me to have the babies. She says, "Your brother and I will have someone to play with while you are in school." I realize later that I should have listened to her.

I kill my unborn babies at Planned Parenthood. Do you not know it is a trick, especially for Black women? Planned Parenthood, founded to exterminate Black babies and reduce our population, is a trick. They brainwash us into thinking women must be pro-choice, but the pro-choice movement still represents murder, depopulation, and sterilization. It is the murder of the miracle of life. My babies would have had babies by now. I would be a grandma. My grandma finds out about the first abortion, but I can never answer her directly when she questions me. Instead, I say, "I can barely take care of myself, so I can't imagine taking care of a baby."

Years later, the guy who insisted I have an abortion goes to my mom's house looking for me. He asks for my phone number, but my mom gives me his number instead. I agree to meet him in person. When he sees me, he says, "You finally grew into that nose." He asks for my number again. I give him a fake number and never speak to him again.

5

Lost

I will seek that which was lost, and bring again that which was driven away, and will bind up that which was broken, and will strengthen that which is sick: but I will destroy the fat and strong; I will feed them with judgment. (Ezekiel 34:16)

At the age of 20, I get my braces removed, start using a new face wash, and look up my hairstylist from childhood, who used to hot press my hair before I got relaxers. I attract a lot of male attention, but I am unprepared for said attention; I am ignorant of their wily ways. I date a string of men who go on to hit me, steal from me, threaten me, yell at me, curse at me, and cheat on me. I pick these men, but I cannot see I am the problem.

I run into a childhood friend who is conflicted about the good and evil of the world. She dabbles a lot in witchcraft using tarot cards, spirit stones, magic spells, love potions, and seeking psychics, but also knows the Bible. She plays with a Ouija board and learns her lesson fast. She conjures spirits through the board, and the spirits want her child.

"What do you mean they wanted your child?"

"They wanted my child. They asked me if they could have her soul. I told them no. My windows, doors, and cabinets were violently closing and opening

9

as I was using the board. It was scary. I had to bury it. Don't ever play with Ouija boards."

She casts spells on her boyfriend through food and articles of his clothing. She speaks about astral travel and shapeshifting. She says the Bible warns us against taking the mark of the beast, and soon they will force it on us; we will not be able to buy or sell without it. She's not taking the mark. She says yoga is evil; its foundation and poses are built on a religion worshipping many false gods, leaving you vulnerable to demonic spirits, similar to those of the Ouija board.

Witchcraft is real. She is trying to warn me, but I don't realize how dangerous it is to associate with people who summon spirits until later.

Kicked out of college with no money, I look for a job, any job. Grandma and Papa buy me a car, so I can get to work. I work part-time doing customer service and eventually move to the east side of the hood in Phoenix, which is considered a safe area. I move into an apartment with a girl I meet at the same job. We go out to a club in Scottsdale every Saturday, and through His mercy, I make it home safe while driving drunk. No DUI, no car accidents *yet*, no tickets, no deaths by car. She will always tell me how funny I am WHEN I AM DRUNK. I will never see her again after I move out of that apartment.

The Holy Spirit knocks some sense into me. I crash the car Grandma and Papa bought me, totaling the car while driving home from work, after falling asleep at the wheel. No alcohol is involved, and no one else is involved. This is the Holy Spirit telling me to go home after refusing to talk to my grandma. I have accused her of trying to control my life (at least, it feels this way in my head). Besides, I miss my papa, too. The Holy

Spirit also convinces me to get an HIV test at the free clinic. I can remember how fast my heart was racing while waiting for the results. The counselor sees the anxiety written on my face and tells me, "I have nothing but good news for you – your results came back negative." God spares my life, but it is a warning.

I swallow my pride and move into my grandparents' house to afford my new Nissan Sentra car payment as well as my credit card and student loan debts. It is a blessing in disguise. After several failed attempts (i.e., flunking out at multiple community colleges), I eventually enroll in a Computer Information Systems Bachelor's Degree Program at a private school. I move into my new apartment six months later and find a part-time job at a transportation and logistics company. I do not have a computer at home, so one night after my shift ends, I work on my résumé in the Industrial Engineering office, but it gets stuck in the printer. The next thing I know, the IE manager offers me a job as a full-time Web Developer. God unstuck my résumé in the printer for the manager to see it. I work for that company for six years, and later, they pay for the remainder of my Bachelor's of Science degree. It is the start of a very successful IT career. Thank God that this manager saw potential in me and gave me a chance.

6

Love

Husbands, love your wives, even as Christ also loved the church,
and gave himself for it.
(Ephesians 5:25)

By the grace of God, I meet a wonderful man studying at the same private school, and we elope in Las Vegas eight months after meeting in the library. He is 21; I am 25. He is such a handsome man with dark, wavy hair and a lean physique from a small town. His face is perfectly symmetrical. I have never seen cuter baby pictures. Unfortunately, he is an innocent bystander in my pierced life full of holes of sorrow. The marriage ends in divorce almost three years later. He doesn't do anything wrong; I am a bad wife. When it doesn't work with him, I know I have a lot of internal work to do. However, had I not met him at that time, I do not know where I would be right now: dead, jail, prostitution, addicted to drugs? I remember him distinctly throwing out a full bottle of prescription Vicodin pills prescribed to me after getting my wisdom teeth pulled, after I rave about how good the drugs make me feel. I believe God sent him to comfort me, give me the love a man should give his wife, the way God loves the church, but I was too stupid to appreciate him. I ask him to forgive me years later. He is now remarried and living a happy life with his wife and children.

7

Willful Sin

Whosoever abideth in him sinneth not: whosoever sinneth hath not seen him, neither known him. (1 John 3:6)

I spend the next few years building my self-esteem, upgrading to better IT jobs. I start a stint in the banking industry that will last almost two decades. I buy my first house, a three-bedroom, two-and-a-half-bath home in the hood, and start dating a coworker. I do not like him much because he is a mean drunk; he calls the woman serving him drinks at a club a cunt. He reminds me of my maternal grandfather, who would always call Mama vile names when he was drunk, which sometimes escalated to physical violence with my aunts. The only thing worse than an old, angry drunk is a young, angry drunk. He calls me a cock tease because I won't put out. So, I start dating his friend.

His friend is intelligent, polite, sophisticated, and never sloppy. He likes to write mathematical proofs on napkins. It's heartwarming that he calls everyone by my name. Instead of calling his mom "Mom", he calls her Dawn. When he talks to his friends, he calls them Dawn. He calls our coworkers Dawn; his angry drunk friend – Dawn. My colleague calls them Twofer, a term she coins meaning two men for the price of one.

14

THE DEVIL'S CONCUBINE

Twofer #1 is the angry drunk, and Twofer #2 is his sophisticated friend. My relationship with Twofer #2 implodes. Not because of the multiple red flags I ignored initially but because he moves to another state to take care of his ailing dad. Twofer #2 admits he cannot introduce me to his dad; he is afraid his dad will die of a heart attack when he sees I am Black. I find a handwritten letter to a friend in prison that reads he is dating a Black woman but not to worry because "I use condoms." He's a mama's boy and relies on her to call him every morning to wake him up for work. I find his profile on a dating site; he's a smoker, and he's racist. I arrive at happy hour when Twofer #1 yells at me, "How dare you show your face here? What you had with [Twofer #2] was fake. It was not a real relationship." Twofer #1 is right. I learn my lesson: do not date a man, then date his friend.

I eventually sell the first house and buy my second house in a safer part of town, in addition to my dream car – a Corvette. My new job is still on the IT side of banking.

8

Therapy

For the lips of a strange woman drop as a honeycomb, and her
mouth is smoother than oil:
But her end is bitter as wormwood, sharp as a two-edged sword.
(Proverbs 5:6-7)

I start therapy. My racist boyfriend says I need a
shrink; I have a cutting tongue. He always reminds me:
looks attract, but personality keeps. So, I do therapy to
save our relationship. I am so ignorant and misguided,
I don't realize it. But the psychologist uncovers the
crux of my imbalance. My relationship with my racist
boyfriend is a symptom of my chaos. She asks about
my mother.

"I have not talked to my mom in 10 years. My
mom forsook[1] me when I was 25, the same year I got
married. I told my mom I wanted her to press charges
against the family member who committed the worst
offense one could commit against my brother, who was
about 5 years old at the time. It happened while we
were living in separate households. There is a police
report. So why not press charges? She told me she
would not and she had a lot on her plate right now. I
say, when he is older, he will resent you for not doing

---

[1] Forsook is past tense for forsake - to leave or abandon.

16

more to prosecute. My grandma recommended not to do anything either; she said, let God handle it. She did not want the other family members retaliating against me or worse. So, I let it go. A few days later, my mom changed her phone number without giving me the new number. She also changed the locks to her front door, which had been the same locks since high school. She eventually put my brother in a group home. My mom was struggling with other tribulations and could not manage my brother's new reality. His trauma at the hands of a family member was so great it manifested itself as severe psychological deficiencies, knocking on the door of a psychosis that only God could fix."

"Have you tried to visit her in person?"

"Why should I go to her house? She changed her phone number and changed the locks. She does not want to talk to me."

The therapist is concerned about the severity of detachment I have towards my mom.

I assure her that my paternal grandparents are active in my life and played a significant role in my upbringing.

"How did your paternal grandparents help raise you?"

"I stayed with them off and on over the years, a few times when I was younger and a few times as a young adult."

"What about your dad?"

"My dad took no interest in me during my formative years. I rarely saw him even though we lived in the same city. I do not know him, and he does not know me. He never attended any event of mine until my college graduation. He missed grammar school and high school events. When I do see him, it is brief, but long enough to drop a gem or two."

"What about your maternal grandparents?"

"I don't see them much either. There was too much trauma when I was very young. My grandfather was a violent and verbally abusive drunk and a smoker. My mom and I lived with them for some time until one night when I saw the devil in his eyes. He made me sit in the dark for hours, terrorizing me while Mama was at church and Mom was at work. He never put his hands on me, but psychologically I was battered. I moved in with my other grandparents that night till my mom found a new place. I saw him once after that night. I didn't attend his funeral years later. Some family members hated me because I skipped it."

"Was there anyone in the family you could trust?"

"Yes, my papa was nice. He did not focus entirely on my looks. He did not yell at me or make me feel stupid. He always spoke words of encouragement. Grandma said I was the apple of Papa's eye.

On the other hand, when I was living with my mom, my grandma would call me every day and ask,

'How is your face?'

'How are your teeth?'

'How is your hair?'

I had a face full of pimples, crooked teeth, and short hair. I had beautiful, long hair up till the age of 13 when my mom took me to the salon and had the lady chop it off and straighten it with a chemical relaxer. I looked like a tomboy in addition to being looks-challenged. It was exhausting having to talk about my insecurities every day for decades. Papa always gave me kisses on the cheek, but my grandma stopped because of those things on my face."

18

THE DEVIL'S CONCUBINE

To clarify, I ask Grandma, "When you say those things, do you mean pimples?"

"Yes."

This recurring theme continued well into my early thirties until I figured out how to get clear skin naturally.

(I now know as an adult my grandma only had the best intentions for me. She knew the world could be cruel and superficial when you're different, not loving and caring like our Lord and Savior. She wanted to save me from the hurts of the world.)

"What about your cousins?"

"I used to be close to my maternal cousins, but not anymore. My favorite cousin was too embarrassed to take me around her friends or even allow me to be at her wedding. She did not want to hang out with anyone who looked like me. When I was 12, she told me she would be too busy to spend time with me since she was married. She always wanted a little sister, but I was too ugly for her.

When she learned she had a half-sister who went to my high school a few years later, she completely abandoned me. My family welcomed the half-sister. Years later, I saw my cousin hiding in the bushes trying to catch her cheating husband in the act, like in the TV series *Cheaters*. Years later, I saw her again at my beloved Papa's funeral. The first thing she said was how pretty I am and she cried, overwhelmed with guilt, apologizing for all the hurt she caused by abandoning me. She said all of this while standing in front of the casket.

Papa visited me in my dreams a few days after he passed away to say thank you for taking care of him and grandma. He said, 'I could always depend on you.'

It warmed my heart and gave me solace while I grieved."

"You have experienced a lot of abandonment, ridicule, and trauma at the hands of the people who are supposed to love you most."

"Yes, I have."

"What about your friends?"

"I have a few good friends, but they are either traveling or live out of town."

I faithfully attend every appointment and discuss my relationship issues and childhood trauma. I am finally able to tap into the suppressed emotions that are imploding – destroying me from the inside out. I have built a wall and cut off part of my brain that processes emotions, but now the emotional floodgates are open. The psychologist helps me work through my trauma and gives me recommendations on how to get healthy physically, mentally, and emotionally. I start exercising. I start riding my bicycle and roller skating again – two of my all-time favorite activities. I read books she recommends. I journal. A few months later, I stop seeing her because I think she is rude for yawning several times during every one of our sessions. I call her out on it, and she says one cannot control yawning. Correct, but you can control how wide you open your mouth when yawning, right? She calls me a few times after I dismiss her, but I never return her calls. She knows I am in serious need of therapy still. I am a ticking time bomb. If only I had been as savage in relationships with men as I am with her.

I meet a new guy while out at a club in Scottsdale, and he's a doctor. I'm with my paternal cousin. I do not go clubbing with her anymore because she leaves without me. It is best to leave together, but she usually does not want to stay, and I am never ready to go. The doctor and I share a common interest – Corvettes. He collects vintage Corvettes and has two in his garage at his six-bedroom house in Scottsdale. We date for a bit until he cancels a date twice for no good reason. He also keeps asking me out on Thursday night dates when he knows I have to work Fridays. I keep running into him in and around town, at the casino, and coincidentally at the Los Angeles International Airport, on a return flight to Arizona after I visit my racist boyfriend in Southern California. (By this time, my ex's father has died. So now, in his mind, it is OK to meet his sister and mom.) The doctor sits next to me on the plane and tells me he wants me to have his baby. He will pay for everything and take care of all the baby's financial needs.

"What about my needs?"

"I will pay for your needs, too."

"To have your baby, we would need to have the same last name; we would need to be married."

"Why do we need to get married?"

"I just told you. You want to use me."

"No, baby. That's not it."

But that was it. A man who wants to have a baby with you but does not want to marry you is a user and a taker. And the entire time we date each other, he never calls me by my name. Instead, he calls me "baby" to avoid calling me by another woman's name, because he has too many women in rotation.

I visit a roller skating rink in Mesa called Skateland. I hit it off with the skaters immediately. One of the guys invites a bunch of us to his house for the Super Bowl. After he introduces me to everyone, his wife's friends start murmuring to her while looking at me, and, without shame, say, "I would not let my husband have friends that look like her." Later, the husband sends me a text message inviting me to visit him and his wife. It'll just be the three of us. The Holy Spirit tells me it is not an invitation for just dinner. I never go to their house again.

I start riding my bicycle more. Initially, I ride it in my neighborhood during the day and start feeling such a flood of endorphins. I switch to riding my bike every night, 10 miles a session. I even purchase a new bike and install monkey lights on the spokes. The lights make my bike look like a spaceship. I start feeling better about my life choices, but start spiraling out of control again.

I wake up in a hotel room wearing a vomit-covered $200 dress the morning after a wild New Year's celebration that I cannot remember. I see missed calls from my grandma. My heart sinks as I listen to her voicemail. I can hear it in her voice she is so worried about me. I called her asking to be picked up from a club the night before. I was either drugged or blacked out because I took too many Patron shots. No, I was drugged; the sober me would never ask my grandma to pick me up from anywhere, not so late at night. And especially because she would worry so much and start calling everyone on speed dial, telling them what happened. The last thing I remember is the guy asking to buy me and my friend a drink. He orders and hands it to her, and she gives it to me. And this is the last thing I remember. Never again would I go to that hotel or that club. Thank God I was not alone.

When I wake up, my friend is also with me. She does not remember anything. She would always tell me, "I have never seen you drunk." Does she see me now? Yes. And she never asks me again. I call my grandma and assure her I am fine and my car is fine. This low point is the impetus for finding God. Because at that time, he had his hand on me; he covered me with His blood. That night could have ended differently, but I survived to tell the story.

9

Ghost

He will turn again, he will have compassion upon us; he will subdue our iniquities; and thou wilt cast all their sins into the depths of the sea. (Micah 7:19)

One day out of the blue, my mom calls me. When I hear her voice, I cry. Her voice is stoic, devoid of emotion. We meet for lunch a few days later, and she fills me in on what has been happening with her during the past decade. She notices my straight teeth, my clear skin, and my eyeshadow.

"Let's talk about the past 10 years you were gone. Do you know how that hurt me? My 'friend' would laugh at me when I told her I had not talked to you in so long."

I am not satisfied with the initial answer she gives me that day.

A few months later, she leaves me a voicemail apologizing for abandoning me. I call her back immediately and ask, "Why not just get me on the phone instead of leaving a voicemail for something so important?" She apologizes again, and I ask her again, "So why did you not contact me all this time?"

"I had too much on my plate dealing with your brother."

This answer triggers me immediately.

24

THE DEVIL'S CONCUBINE

"What do you mean? I was an obedient child. I never gave you any problems. My brother (of legal age now) curses at you, threatens you, and has put his hands on you, and you turn your back on *me*?"

She has no response.

"Do you love me?"

She says, "Of course, I love you. Why do you always ask me that question?"

"I started questioning your love when I was 14 years old, when my friend Jane called me at the house. And you said to her, 'Hold on, sweetie,' before you handed me the phone. Why did you never call me 'sweetie'? My brother, my friend – a girl you didn't know and hadn't met, and others in the family, but never me did you call 'sweetie'."

"You do not seem like the sweetie type."

"Look, I know my brother is your favorite, and I am OK with it."

"I do not play favorites. I love both of you equally."

"The Bible says parents have favorites."

I continued, "What did you tell your side of the family when they asked about me? Did they ask about me?"

"I told them you were doing fine."

"You told them I was doing fine, even though you hadn't talked to me for years?"

"Are you going to keep reminding me of my past?"

"You are right. I will never bring it up again, ever. I will pray God throws these memories into the sea of forgetfulness."

The pain still lingers. Later, I realize no answer will pacify my broken heart until I find Jesus.

I run into my little brother while shopping in Tempe, and the encounter leaves me at a crossroads.

25

He no longer lives in a group home. Instead, he lives on the streets despite having opportunities to live in an apartment and means to pay his rent. I take him to lunch and tell him how much I love him and I'm sorry I wasn't there to protect him when he was little. He says, "It's not your fault, sister. I'll be OK." Later, I ask my mom if it is OK for him to live with me. She says no because he can be violent. My grandma tells me no because he will steal from me. Others tell me no because his street life friends will follow him to my home. If only I had known what was to come many years later, I might have made a different decision.

10

Wayward

Lest thou shouldest ponder the path of life, her ways are moveable, that thou canst not know them. (Proverbs 5:6)

A few years later, I go to San Francisco on business and for the yearly Christmas party. The company rents out Ruby Skye, a two-story nightclub in Union Square, which is now a church ironically. At the end of the party, my manager asks me if I want to get some pizza across the street. He says he wants to be sure I make it back to the hotel safely. I am staying at the Hyatt Regency at the Embarcadero. I naively allow him into my hotel room, where I quickly figure out I have made a mistake.

"I don't share cock," I say.

He is married with kids. I am so proud that I have turned him down, but I know it could have ended badly. I need to be more careful. He calls me a few days later and apologizes.

"I hope my actions don't get in the way of our working relationship."

"No, they will not but please don't bring this up again. I want to forget this happened."

That year, I receive my highest bonus and salary increase since starting at the bank, but our work relationship is doomed to fail. I work in that role for a few more years, participating in many diversity and inclusion programs and opportunities for minorities to develop and hone technical and leadership skills, until I grow tired of him. And the feeling is mutual. I complete a survey telling the company they should invest heavily in manager training because sexual harassment is rampant at the bank. Soon after, he becomes a real jerk, which gives me the perfect excuse to move to another position within the company. I can sue, but no, I am way too happy with my paycheck and want to continue working on the IT side of banking.

I learn later it is an unspoken rule that you do not snitch on managers at this particular bank. Another manager (also married) tries me at a different work function by slapping my butt, and I reject him, too. I cannot prove it, but I think he charged over $150 in liquor expenses to my hotel room because he was so salty. I dispute the fraudulent charges, and the hotel removes them from my bill.

I move into a new role reporting to a woman I attended high school with, who I don't remember. She reminds me she knew me in high school, attempts to fire me, and then tells me she is worried about me slashing her tires. She fails miserably. I stay in my current role, and she gets demoted to a non-manager role. The Head of my department intervenes on my behalf because the work I did before that role was exceptional, garnering many cash bonuses, recognition, and merit increases. My bitter ex-manager is still scratching her head because God had other plans for me.

I return to San Francisco six years later, under new management, for another Christmas party. I meet a man so handsome he looks like he can be on the cover

of *GQ* magazine. He is a cross between Joe
Manganiello and Brad Paisley. Frankly, he is out of my
league: thick, black, wavy hair, beautiful eyes, olive
skin, tall, thin. I send my mom a picture of him, and
she says, "Do not introduce him to any of your
friends." First red flag – he has a girlfriend.

For giggles, I present the ugly duckling matrix. (Do
not come for me. I am poking fun at myself. It's
called healing.)

How do you know you were an ugly duckling and
possibly a little ugly as an adult? You can relate to the
scenarios in the Ugly Duckling Matrix.

Ugly Duckling Matrix

1. When your granduncle says, "You have to be careful. Men are going to want to talk to you because you have a pretty car." (I was driving a Corvette at the time.)
2. When you see a family member at the grocery store, who you haven't seen since you were 11, and they cannot stop hugging you and gushing about how pretty you are *now*.
3. When your friend's mom says to you, "You look like a girl *now*."
4. When your father tells your grandma, "I didn't realize Dawn was *that* cute."
5. When your mother tells you not to introduce your friends to a man you like.
6. While washing your hands in the bathroom at the club, the bathroom attendant says, "With the right makeup, you can have any man you want."
7. When a restaurant manager you have seen a few times before, while accompanying your grandparents for lunch, always asks about you, and your grandma says, "He must have fallen in love with your voice when you called him that one time." (I cut my hair into a teeny, tiny afro, and Grandma did not like my new look.)
8. When you show a photo of your work crush to your mom, and she says, "Be careful."

A few years later, I see GQ again, same place –
Ruby Skye. Different girlfriend.

He says, "How long has it been? Six years?"
"Yes."

He says, "Each year, I wonder if you are going to
show up."

He continues, "You have not changed much. Your
hair has more volume. You are one of the best-looking
women in here."

"Do you have a girlfriend now? Are you married?"
"I am seeing someone."

We quickly catch up. He tells me what he has been
up to, and so do I. I notice his coworkers are not
standing next to us anymore. They've gone downstairs.
GQ and I are alone.

I ask him, "What is there to do around here?"

"Union Square is right down the street. There are
bars all over the place."

"Are you going to show me around town tonight?"

He says he is going to hang out with his coworkers
later to smoke a j. I ask if he is going to invite me.
He says it is not his stuff to smoke, so he cannot invite
me. Whatever. I tell him he still looks handsome.

He pays me a compliment also, but I cannot
remember what he said. Cut to closing time. He asks
me for my phone number. He hugs me, and we go our
separate ways. I go to get my coat from the coat check.
I start walking back to Hotel Nikko when a short guy
approaches me and asks me if I want to go to an afterparty. He looks harmless, and I am not doing anything
else. So, I ask where the afterparty is. It is at some
restaurant. I agree to go, and we start walking. I see
GQ. He tells me he sent me a text message.

"Why did you not respond?"

"I did not get the text message. My cell provider sucks."

GQ says he talked to his coworkers, and they are cool with me hanging with them. I tell the short guy, "Maybe I will see you later. But I am going to leave with [GQ]."

GQ laughs.

"Wow, you have perfect timing. I was about to go with homeboy, and then you swooped in."

"I saw that. If the guy looked like me, I would have left you alone, but that guy is not me."

Damn right, he is not like you, I thought. At all.

GQ, his friends, and I go to Union Square. We smoke a j. His friends leave. GQ and I decide to hang out at the bar across the street from the hotel. He orders whiskey on the rocks. I order Riesling. I try the whiskey, and it is terrible. He tells me a story about his grandpa. His grandpa says, "Beware of a woman who likes whiskey."

GQ says, "My grandpa was right about women."

We talk for hours, and it's fun. I ask about his girlfriend, but he does not talk about her much. I tell him, I need to ask you about her to keep myself honest. My mind is starting to wander. He smiles and says, "Now, why do we need to talk about that?" I let it go.

We leave the bar and hear blues music. It is coming from a bar across the street. We go there; he orders another whiskey, and I order water. An attractive girl sits at the bar alone eating a salad. He chats her up. A few minutes later, he is still chatting her up. I get pissed off and leave. As I walk away from the bar toward the hotel, I wonder how he could be so rude to talk to another girl while he is with me. It pisses me off. What an ass. I get to the hotel, and the doors are locked. How am I supposed to get to my room? Do I need to walk around the entire block alone to find the entrance to this place? It's not safe to walk alone at 1 a.m. I turn around and head back to the bar where I left him. The girl is still sitting at the bar, but he is not there. I wait for a minute. He emerges from the restroom and says, "You left."

I say, "Yes, I left. You were talking to another girl."

"She is waiting for some guy. She is not interested in me."

That is bull. I should not get mad at a guy who is out with me, has a girlfriend, and talks to another girl at the bar.

I tell him I came back because I could not find my way into the hotel. He laughs. I don't.

That night would be the last time GQ and I would hang out. Later, I would run into him everywhere: Trader Joe's, on my lunch break, walking to work. Sometimes we would acknowledge each other with a friendly hello. Other times, there was no acknowledgment because I saw him first, and he did not recognize me in my 'Incognegro' disguise: hair in two braids, a baseball cap, and shades.

11

The Last Supper

And, ye fathers, provoke not your children to wrath: but bring them up in the nurture and admonition of the Lord.
(Ephesians 6:4)

For my fortieth birthday, my father invites me to dinner at Red Lobster. I am excited because this is the first time he has asked me to dinner *ever*, one on one, father and daughter, and I love Red Lobster, so it's a win-win. As I sit across from him at the table, he tells me things I am not ready to hear, but it brings me closer to God because unbeknownst to me, I will have to learn how to forgive him for what he is about to say.

He says, "When you were born, my mom gave you so much love and attention." I bite a piece of garlic bread as he continues.

"But when I was little, mom would ignore me. I would always call out to her, 'Mom, Mom, Mom!' I would call out to her as she was ironing clothes, but she would not respond."

It takes me a minute to understand where he is going, and I ask him, "So, you resented me when I was born because I got the attention that your mom did not give you?"

"No. That is not what I am saying."

"What are you saying then?"

34

"I am saying that when you were born, Papa and Mama loved you so much and showered you with attention. And I thought, wow, this is very different from my upbringing."

"Why did you wait 40 years to tell me this story? I did not ask to be born. I didn't do anything wrong."

"I wanted you to know."

"I had a hard time as a child, and because of Grandma and Papa, I grew up to be a civilized, successful member of society. My mother may have had her issues, but she tried the best she could. What she could not do for me, Grandma and Papa did for me. But you did nothing for me."

"I gave you half of my genetic makeup."

"What an arrogant answer! I didn't ask for a parent who couldn't love me due to his broken childhood, insecurity, and maladjustment. This story explains why you were absent from my life, during the worst parts of my life when I needed you most. During the ugly-duckling phase, the formative years, when the kids at school and even family members made fun of the way I looked. Do you know how difficult it was for me as a young girl?"

"Kids can be mean." He continues with a smirk on his face and validates all my insecurities, saying, "You were an odd child. You did not have any friends."

At that moment, I lose it. In a voice too loud for a restaurant, I said, "Why are you validating all of my insecurities? How dare you say these things to me? Who invites their daughter to dinner to insult her? Why are you not congratulating me for my accomplishments and telling me how proud you are that I graduated college, and I'm working? What is wrong with you?"

35

"It is good that you found a career."

"What is that supposed to mean?"

"You are on the obsessive-compulsive spectrum."

"You are not a doctor. How can you diagnose someone when you have no credentials? You don't know me. You have no idea who I am. We don't even talk to each other."

"I trained in the field, so I know."

I don't remember the conversation after this moment. The last thing I hear before leaving the restaurant is, "Dawn, you know I love you."

I sit in my car for what seems like an eternity, unable to speak, unable to cry, unable to start the car to drive. I am in shock. How can a father resent his daughter? What kind of man waits 40 years to clear his conscience for being an absent father?

The dinner conversation breaks my heart again. The little girl inside me cries again. I relive her pain again. The magnitude of that conversation is so devastating to my heart that it draws me closer to my mom. God softens my heart that night, and I start to forgive my mom for abandoning me. I need someone to help me deal with this new pain, and my mom can help me through it. God, now I understand why you waited so long to bring my mom back into my life when I needed her most. You have perfect timing.

God also shows me that my father had a chance to redeem his parental iniquities with me, by loving my other little brother from his second marriage the way his parents didn't love him. And his parents loved me the way their son could not love me. It was all in the Lord's divine appointment. The Lord knew my father's heart and filled my life with love from Grandma and Papa and not my father's resentment.

But it would be a few more years until I could forgive him, until my breakthrough, because God was still working on me.

12

The Devil's Concubine

*For the commandment is a lamp; and the law is light and
reproofs of instruction are the way of life:
To keep thee from the evil woman, from the flattery of the tongue
of a strange woman.
Lust not after her beauty in thine heart neither let her take thee
with her eyelids. (Proverbs 6:23-25)*

I start traveling solo that same year to escape:
Hawaii for a week, Mexico for eight days, and the
Caribbean for seven days. I overcome many fears
traveling solo. I am no longer afraid of heights. I am
no longer afraid of talking to strangers. I am no longer
afraid of water. I am no longer afraid of eating alone. I
am no longer afraid of going to the movies alone. I am
no longer afraid of going on vacation alone. I am no
longer afraid.

Then my grandma passes away, and my relationship
with my paternal family is never the same. My
grandma spends the last month of her life in the
hospital. On the day she is admitted, she calls me and
says she doesn't want anyone in her room except me.
So, I do what any obedient granddaughter should do
and ask my cousins to leave when I arrive in her room.
They think it's me not wanting them to see her, but she

wants peace in her room, not chaos. I try to explain it to my cousins, but they do not believe me.

I slip away to San Francisco to grieve for a week. My grandma was my biggest intercessor.[2] We talked almost every day, and now she's gone to see the Lord with Papa. I am alone. I miss her so much that she appears in my dreams and tells me to stop crying, to which I respond with more crying; then she looks at me and says in her "you're in trouble" tone, "Dawn, Dawn." I cry myself awake. I stay in a luxurious room at the Clift Hotel, where I meet a woman in the Redwood Room (the hotel bar). She asks if I am a model. No, I am not. Either way, she wants me to be her muse and to introduce me to her friend, who is always looking for different types to model her clothing line. We exchange numbers. She is a stunning woman, a professional model who resembles Audrey Hepburn.

It's a short-lived friendship with many adventures. We have a great time on the town, dancing, karaoke, getting free drinks, and singing backup for a local band at Swig. We are a one-hit-wonder, singing "Mustang Sally" for the crowd. Audrey tells me that every night a ghost knocks on her front door and stands in the doorway, saying nothing when she opens the door.

"A ghost?"

"Yes, a ghost; he haunts the building." (Audrey lives in an old 1920s building in the Tendernob.)

It is a funny story, and I think she is joking, till I spend the night at her place; the short-term rental is not available for move-in till the next day. I ask her the next morning if her ghost friend visited her last night while I was asleep.

---

[2] An intercessor is a person who prays to God on behalf of another person.

"Yes."

"Really? Because I didn't hear anything."

She casually drops into the conversation that she is a witch and practices levitation with her friends. RED FLAG!

Later, Audrey meets a guy, and we all decide to go back to his place. I am tired and tell her I want to leave, but before I leave, she tries to get me to stay, grabs me, and kisses me on my forehead. The Holy Spirit tells me she is looking to have fun tonight.

"Sorry, I need to go home. The bed is calling me."

She asks if I have any condoms.

"No, please don't have sex with him without a condom. Go to the store. Protect yourself." And I leave.

I check on her the next day and ask if she is OK. She says she is fine. They had sex but did not use a condom.

"Are you afraid of catching a disease?"

"No, I am lucky."

I realize I did to her what my paternal cousin did to me when she left me at a club. I left my friend alone at a strange man's house. I am a horrible friend.

One night we go to the Starlight Room for late-night dancing inside of Sir Francis Drake Hotel. It is a lounge on the top floor, and it overlooks the city. At close, they play Tony Bennett's "I Left my Heart in San Francisco." I know then that I want to make SF my home, but I will no longer befriend her. She admits that she will choose her other friend over me because she's known him longer and his pockets are deep. OK. Deuces.

I return a few months later and get a modest room at the Burritt Hotel for another weeklong stay. My first outing is SF Jazz to see Chris Botti in concert. A modern-day, handsome older man with a nicely manicured beard introduces himself to me while I wait for a Lyft. He is a clean-cut version of Grizzly Adams from the old '80s TV series, and he works for SF Jazz, providing transportation for musicians to and from the venue. He asks for my number, and we meet a few days later for coffee at Caffe Trieste and dinner at Tommaso's in North Beach. He tells me the story of "OMing" - Orgasmic Meditation. There is a club in the city called OneTaste that allows women to be stroked sexually by strangers only after fully consenting. He invites me for a nightcap, but I quickly get out of there. This is the last night I see him. My spidey senses are improving.

Back at Burritt, I go down to the hotel lobby for live jazz. I sit at the bar next to a woman who looks like a younger version of Apollonia from the movie *Purple Rain*. She tells me she can show me around since I am new to the city. We exchange numbers and hang out a few days later. We go to Public Works for house music. The problem is Apollonia takes something before we get to the club, and once when we arrive, she is sloppy. So sloppy that I have to get us into a Lyft to take her home because the men start to notice, too, and try to convince us to hang out with them. During the ride home, the song "Maria" from *West Side Story* is on the radio, and she starts singing at the top of her lungs. The Lyft driver gets annoyed and turns off the radio. I hope we don't get kicked out of his car. We arrive at her place, and she asks me to spend the night with her because she does not want to be alone. The Holy Spirit tells me she wants to do more than sleep. "No. I am

leaving." I call another Lyft to get back home. I call
her the next day.

"Do you remember what happened?"

"No, what happened?"

"You could hardly walk. You were belligerent, loud,
flirting, and kissing random men. It was difficult for
me to take care of you. What drugs did you take last
night?"

"I did not take any drugs."

(Yeah. Right.)

"I cannot hang out with you anymore when you
abuse drugs because you put both our lives at risk."

I learned my lesson previously at the forgetful New
Year's celebration and did not drink that night. This
should have been the last time I spoke to Apollonia.

I fly back to Arizona but don't stay long. I hire a
landscaper to tend to my yard, install a Ring security
doorbell, give a spare key to a friend, plug my car into a
battery saver in the garage, and take off to San
Francisco for four months – the entire summer. I sign
a lease for a furnished, short-term rental for over
$3,000 a month in Nob Hill. I remember the first few
weeks, getting accustomed to the nightlife and the
logistics of getting groceries without having a car and
the walking commute to work up and down California
Street. I hang out with Apollonia at her new place.
She introduces me to all of her friends. We go to
concerts and meet for dinner at her favorite restaurant
in The Mission. Life in San Francisco is fantastic. I
invite her to go to the Italian Jazz Festival in North
Beach, but she has another idea. She meets me at my
tiny studio, and we walk to Park Tavern – a nice Italian
restaurant across from Washington Square Park – for
lunch. I tell her about Jesus, but she does not believe

in Jesus. I tell her how if it was not for Him, I would not be here, but she changes the subject.

A friend of hers, who is a local realtor, joins us later after lunch. We go to a second spot to have a quick bite of pizza at Tony Napoletana – the best pizza in San Francisco. The pizza is delicious. We also order wine, and it is a good time. He invites us both to his place. We eat a few loaded cookies, drink a little more, and listen to music – Journey, Stevie Wonder, Jill Scott. We are comfortable on his bed. Fellatio ensues, but he chooses not to come, and she is upset. After hours of drinking and waiting for the cookies to take effect, she passes out to his right, and he turns to me on his left.

"Do you want to have sex?"

"No, she likes you."

He stares into my eyes for hours, chatting and trying to convince me to sleep with him. Throughout the night, she goes in and out of wakefulness. (I had been drinking a lot, too, but I discovered a way to stay sober no matter what or how much I consume. Before a night on the town, I drink a tablespoon of olive oil.) He finally stops asking for sex, turns his back towards me, and cuddles with her. We sleep for a few hours and wake up around 6 a.m., but it is too early for Lyft to pick us up. We awkwardly wait around until we get confirmation that a Lyft is on the way. Lyft drops us off at my pad, and she drives herself home. I tell her later that he tried to have sex with me, but I refused his advances. All she talks about is how upset she is that he did not ejaculate. Things could have ended differently that night too, but I lived to tell the story.

Shortly after, Apollonia and I stop hanging out. The time between sending a text and receiving a text turns into hours, then days. Until one day, the communication ends, which should have been the last day I talked to her.

I see a post on Facebook for Thursday night – a jazz band is performing live. I love jazz! I arrive at the venue and find a small, cozy lounge with performers to the right of the door. I locate a seat, notice the DJ behind his stand, and our eyes lock. He is a tall, handsome man with beautiful eyes and dark hair. A few songs later, he comes over, introduces himself, and asks for my phone number. Cut to the end of the night, and I tell him I'm leaving. He grabs me for a hug, but first, he slowly takes my face into both his hands and gently kisses me. He puts my head on his chest and holds me tight while we stand in the middle of the dancefloor. It is like time stops, and we are the only two on the dancefloor under the spotlight. The entire crowd is watching us. It is magical.

He calls and plans a date for Saturday. We decide to meet for drinks at Rye. It is amazing. We have Indian food at Chutney and more drinks at Bourbon and Branch. We go to a jazz lounge. We dance a few songs, then he leaves briefly to use the restroom. When the DJ returns, he finds me talking with the manager. The manager offers me a job there as a hostess and gives me his number. I introduce the DJ to the manager, and as soon as he leaves, the DJ says, "I leave you alone for a second, and you are talking to another man?" I tell him he asked if I wanted to work there. I later learn the manager likes men.

The DJ calls again and asks me out on another date for the following weekend. He arrives wearing a hat, an Italian shirt, jeans, and shoes. The man and his clothes – Italian. I love the way he dresses and the way he smells, but he is 45 minutes late. I tell him I cannot go out with him because he does not respect my time. He is 6 foot 4, with dark hair, a beard, and cute dimples. He has a beautiful face, but I do not trust him. He apologizes profusely and says he's mortified. He stares into my eyes for an eternity, it seems. As I tell him to leave, my voice cracks. It pains me to cancel our date because he is late, but I want him to respect me. On his way out, he says to call him when I want to see him again.

I call him a week later, and we meet again. This time he is on time. I meet him at Tabletop. We stare into each other's eyes for hours in the middle of the second floor of the bar, faces maybe an inch apart. His pheromones are intoxicating. I ask him what cologne he wears, but he does not wear cologne. People comment on what a beautiful couple we are. He does not like my revealing dress. He calls it lingerie. On the way to our third date, he points out a woman dressed conservatively on the street, as if to scold me and show me how a woman should dress, unlike me, who wears short dresses exposing my cleavage.

We have one more date at a secluded beach in Pacifica, where we have the entire section to ourselves. For lunch, we go to a nice restaurant overlooking the ocean, for ceviche. Here, I inquire about how many women he is seeing; there are several in rotation. He says my walls are up. I think to myself, our dates always span at least 12 hours. But after we say our goodbyes, I don't hear from him unless I reach out first.

We will never get to know each other intimately, and my walls cannot come down. Now that I'm in San Francisco, it is more important than ever to ask a potential suitor to get a 10-panel STD test, and for both of us to share results. The DJ ignores my request – a major red flag.

It's a Sunday night, and I have plans to stay in and be lazy, but I am restless. My upstairs neighbors turn on their music, and the bass is loud. It reverberates through the walls. So, after watching *Big Brother*, I decide to walk to the same jazzy hotel bar and sit in the same seat at the Burritt Room. I look to my left, and there is a man, but he is talking to someone to his left. To my right, there is a couple on a date. I grab the menu but cannot decide which drink to order. The man to my left suggests that I order a Manhattan. (Manhattans are too strong for me.) I smile at him. He has a chiseled face. A beard, very rugged. He looks like a younger, more handsome version of Al Pacino circa *Carlito's Way*. His face is dreamy. A few minutes later, he and his friend decide they are leaving to go to another spot. He invites me to go to the Devil's Acre to listen to jazz.

"Maybe I will see you later," I say.

He smiles and leaves. I order my drink. Malbec. I finish it and call a Lyft. The Lyft driver tells me if I were his granddaughter, he would not want me going to a place called the Devil's Acre. It is God warning me. When I arrive, Manhattan immediately greets me with a smile. We go to the bar, and he orders a drink for me. We talk for hours. His friends are performing, and the music is phenomenal. We have a good conversation. His jazz artist friends finish their set, and Manhattan introduces me to them.

Manhattan introduces me to his friend (the guy sitting to his left at Burritt Room) as well. Manhattan leaves to go to the restroom, and I notice his pants are sagging. What's up with that? I also notice that the

46

bartenders ignore him, and he does not leave a tip. He has a little girl, but he doesn't tell me; his friend does. Manhattan doesn't want me to know he has a daughter because I would glean that he still has a relationship with his baby mama – another red flag, but I ignore the warning signs and spend a lot of time with him over the next few months instead.

Apollonia finally responds to a text originally sent a few days prior.

Here is the letter I wrote to San Francisco that summer while living in Nob Hill. I continue to journal a lot still, but I have replaced bike riding with walking up and down the hilly streets and roller skating at the Church of Eight Wheels – a former church building now used as a roller rink. I am experiencing a lot of turmoil caused by family, self, and life in general. I am preparing to go back to Arizona after an unforgettable summer in the city. I have tears in my eyes as I write my love letter to San Francisco.

SF Got Me Like

SF got me ready to marry a city.

SF summers make me want to sing like Donna Summer's song, "Spring Affair." It is a Spring Affair in the summer in the city of SF. It is so sexy here. The men with their beards, square jaws, soulful eyes. I am mesmerized like the Miguel Migs mix, San Francisco. I walk down the street, and both men and women smile. The men with their nice, shiny shoes. The women in their stiletto heels and flawless makeup and hair. I feel happier in my 360-square-foot studio than I ever have in a 2,060-square-foot home in suburban Arizona. Arizona – where the people look the same, think the same, and act the same.

47

SF, you bring out the good, the tears, the anger – all my emotions. Sometimes it is tears of joy, sometimes heartbreak. I would not trade it for a second. I hope I can stay with you, San Francisco, for a very long time. You make me so happy. This city feeds my soul: your music, your people, your culture, your food, your crooked streets, and your steep hills.

I have met so many exceptional souls here with so many unforgettable adventures.

I fell in love with you 11 years ago. We have so much fun together. There is no one else like you in the world. I cannot imagine leaving you now. Where do I sign on the dotted line? I have a soft spot for your food, your people, your culture, and your vibe. I love you, San Francisco.

Arizona, you suck the life out of my soul. Arizona, it's not you; it's me. Arizona, you distress me. I worry about my home, my car, and my sanity. Arizona is the place where Black people go to die. I've found someone else. Hello, San Francisco.

San Francisco – I only worry about getting enough vitamin D.

Arizona, it is not you; it is me. I have found someone new. San Francisco, you are my true love.

I have to go home soon, back to AZ. Well, AZ no longer feels like my home. I like my home in AZ, but my house is not a home as described in the Luther Vandross song, "A House is Not a Home."

"A house is not a home when there is no one there to hold you tight and no one there you can kiss goodnight. A house is not a

THE DEVIL'S CONCUBINE

*home when the two of us are far apart, and one of us has a
broken heart. I am not meant to live alone. Turn this house into
a home."*

*If I live the remainder of my life alone, I would rather be alone in
San Francisco. I am feeling depressed and have not left SF yet.
I can feel the tears welling up in my eyes. What is it that I will
miss about SF? I will miss the trolley cars going up and down
California Street. I will miss the trolley attendants sounding the
bells. I will miss walking by Grace Cathedral and hearing the
bell toll at the top of the hour. I will miss the walks up and
down the hills. I will miss the smells of weed permeating wherever
I go. I will miss the disco. I will miss the fashion. I will miss
the sun peeking out through the tallest skyscrapers. I will miss
the crooked streets. I will miss eating watermelon in bed. I will
miss ordering food to be delivered straight to my door. I will miss
the friendly people with smiling faces walking their dogs. I will
miss the random people introducing themselves to me. I will miss
the music. I will miss the kisses. I will miss waking up in this
little studio every morning. I will miss the 360-square-foot
apartment. It is so cute.*

SF has changed me. I do not know how to live without you, SF.

*I want to come back, and I have not even left yet. I think it is
time to sell my AZ home and my beloved car. You both deserve
an owner who will be there for you full-time.*

San Francisco, where the police officers smile and say hello.

13

Dead Body

For the wages of sin is death; but the gift of God is eternal life through Jesus Christ our Lord. (Romans 6:23)

The San Francisco honeymoon phase ends abruptly. One morning, I wake up to a loud pounding at my door. It is the San Francisco Fire Department (SFFD). I open the door, and four firefighters are standing before me.

"Can you identify the body of a neighbor who lives a few doors down? She passed away."

"No, I don't know anyone here."

With a condescending tone, "You don't know your neighbors?"

"This unit is a short-term rental. I am only here for a few months."

They apologize and tell me to have a good day. Yeah, right. Through the peephole, I see them roll the deceased woman out of the apartment on a gurney; she's wrapped in a body bag. I text the property manager a few days later to get more information. He assures me it was not a homicide; she died of a heart attack. He is a former police officer, tall, skinny, handsome, and has a cute little Yorkie dog named Hunter that weighs no more than four pounds. He makes EPs and says he is going to write a song about me, but he too has a girlfriend. Does every man I meet in SF have a girlfriend? I think it is a part of the SF game: tell a woman you have a girlfriend, so she knows it's just a fling, even if you're single. I didn't touch that "situationship". The ex-cop says the deceased woman's daughter is coming to retrieve her mom's belongings in a few days. The ugly side of city living hits me in the heart. I get a good strong dose of reality. A few nights before she died, I asked God to send me someone so that I would not die alone. This poor lady died alone.

The next day, the mailman accidentally puts the deceased woman's mail into my mailbox. It is time for me to go back to Arizona. It is creepy here. My friend talks me into staying till October when I tell all my San Francisco buddies goodbye. I am not sure when I will be back, but I want to see Manhattan again.

I see the ex-cop a few years later working security at a Jamiroquai concert. He pretends he doesn't see me. Karl the Fog looks to pay a visit inside the auditorium that night because the plume of weed and other smokable forms of drugs is so thick, which could explain the disturbing dreams I have later that night, possibly due to the secondhand smoke inhalation. I almost say hi as an excuse to ask about Hunter but quickly dismiss the idea. I miss seeing his cute little doggy.

14

Humility

In my distress I called upon the LORD, and cried unto my God: he heard my voice out of his temple, and my cry came before him, even into his ears. (Psalms 18:6)

Manhattan visits me in Arizona quite frequently, but this trip will be his last. We go to The Ostrich for stiff drinks. The guy working the front door talks with me briefly before we get seated. I look around, and Manhattan is not standing next to me. I see him standing across the room with fury in his eyes.

"What is wrong?"

"Why are you talking to that guy like I am not here? He is flirting with you right in front of me. That is so disrespectful."

"You live with a woman you won't leave. You have no right to get angry with me for something you have been doing since day one."

"I told you I am working on leaving her."

Once he learns I am deceiving him for my own selfish needs, he leaves me. The unstable relationship can no longer support lies, deceit, and greed. That's what happens when you live in willful sin.

It is New Year's Eve again. I am home alone again in my cold four-bedroom, two-bathroom house with a den in Arizona, and I am so lonely. My mom is not answering the phone, the few local friends I have are out of town, and no one is around to see my tears. I am alone and hopeless. I call the suicide helpline at 1-800-273-8255. I hang up when the line connects. They call right back even though I blocked my number, but I do not answer. It is at this moment I know I have to get out of Arizona, or I will wither away and die. I cry out to God with my face full of tears. God, please help me! I cry myself to sleep.

For the next few weeks, I start looking for jobs in California. After a three-month-long search, I find a new job with my employer (at the time) in San Francisco. The interviews go so well that the recruiter meets with the Head of Compensation to get approval for my salary increase. I am justified; the cost of living difference between San Francisco and Phoenix is exponential. I text Apollonia to ask if it is OK to contact the realtor because I am interested in buying a condo.

"I would like you to go to someone else rather than him because he is not a good person."

Why did you introduce me to him if he is not a good person? You probably thought we would have a nice threesome, right? I do not bother to ask her. Instead, I find an apartment quickly. I'm officially living in San Francisco now.

My first full day as a San Francisco resident, I walk a few blocks away to order breakfast for takeout. As I wait, I sit down next to a woman who strikes up a conversation with me. When she learns where I work, she asks if I want to meet her husband, who is standing outside and happens to be the CEO of my employer. At this point, my employer is all over the news after a whistleblower exposed deceptive practices against unsuspecting customers. The bank has to pay many fines and answer to many regulators. Its reputation never returns to good standing, but the CEO and his wife seem like kind people despite the controversy.

15

Eyes Wide Shut

As a jewel of gold in a swine's snout, so is a fair woman which is without discretion. (Proverbs 11:22)

The next day, I meet two women at a bank who will test my boundaries. One is tall, lean with long, auburn hair. She looks like a version of the woman described by Dolly Parton in her hit song "Jolene." The other woman is short in stature with short black hair; she wears red lipstick. I see them again at the street corner a few minutes later, and we decide we should hang out. They accompany me to the UPS store, where I have packages waiting for pickup. Once I get to the UPS store, I realize these boxes are way too big for me to get home by myself. The women offer to help because they have a car. It is Jolene's friend's car, a Mercedes E-class. He is letting her use it. We drop off the boxes at my pad and decide to go to a local bar – Pagan's Idol. We take turns buying rounds of drinks, except Jolene. Jolene works her way around the bar, talking to older gentlemen and getting them to buy her drinks. They have to go back home to San Jose that night, so we exchange numbers and go our separate ways. We keep in touch over the next few months via texts and phone calls. Until one day, Jolene says she is visiting San Francisco. We meet at Super Duper Burgers in the

Castro. I know something is wrong when she walks into a burger shop with her luggage.

She tells me about how she was admitted to the psych ward on an emergency three-day hold, where she was molested. She says Red, the other woman in our trio, is the reason she was put there in the first place.

"How did you escape?"

"I threatened to call my lawyer. I am working with my lawyer to have my medical records reviewed and changed."

She says everything in the movie *Eyes Wide Shut* is true. She says if they find that you have contracted a disease, they will murder you. And this is why she is working with her lawyer to get them to change her medical records.

She says she has seen some terrible stuff – people killing their babies so they can live in the United States. I tell her I do not want to hear anything about murdered babies. She changes the subject.

"I am the owner of several businesses, one of which involves charging customers $7,500 an hour for sessions with me to talk about their problems." She shows me a text message from a priest who is one of her clients.

"Do you want to see a dead cat? I have a picture on my phone."

"No."

I am disturbed now, so I change the subject. "How is your friend doing, the guy that loaned you his Mercedes?"

"He is upset because I totaled his car; I had an asthma attack while driving on the freeway. It was a mistake."

56

THE DEVIL'S CONCUBINE

She asks me how I am doing and if I am making friends in the city. I am uncomfortable for some reason. Sort of like she is fishing for something, grasping to find a weakness that she can use against me. Or, maybe she is genuinely concerned. Not! She is fishing for information and, I do not feel comfortable talking about myself after that.

"Why do you have your luggage in tow?"

"I am leaving tonight to travel the world, and my real name is Celestine, not Jolene."

I do not know who this person is. She has at least two aliases; Celestine and Jolene. She starts talking about the KGB. She says the KGB is still in operation.

I must have an awful look on my face or I have crossed my eyes because my contact lens gets stuck at the top of my eye. I excuse myself and run to the restroom and try to push it back into place, but I cannot find it. So, I go back to Celestine/Jolene and tell her I have to leave because my contact lens is lodged at the top of my eye. Once I get home, I can find my lens, and everything is back to normal, but I never speak to her again after that discussion. I need to be more careful. I see Red once more. She picks me up, and we go to Black Sands Beach in Sausalito. She mentions that she and Jolene used to date. I never see Red after that day. Red and I correspond through email till we eventually lose contact.

Several years later, I receive a text message from Red's phone: "Tell Red that [her boyfriend] filed a police report for all the horrible things she did to him. She's now in the system forever, which is what a monster like her deserves." Someone has accessed Red's phone and spammed her contacts with links to videos of her assaulting her estranged boyfriend.

I often think about Jolene/Celestine and Red but have decided to leave them in the hands of God.

16

Death Bed

The LORD shall fight for you, and ye shall hold your peace.
(Exodus 14:14)

Two weeks later, I get a call from my maternal cousin. My little brother (my mom's son) is in the hospital, and he will most likely die. He's had a stroke and cannot talk – only moan. I cannot go back to Arizona; I have just started my new job. I try to make sense of the situation. My brother's legal guardian has tried to kill him via neglect by dispensing the wrong medication, which gave him a stroke?

"Yes. We need a lawyer to get the family emergency guardianship. If he remains in the state's care, they will let him die," my cousin says.

My cousin finds a lawyer for a $5,000 retainer. I do not have money to give with the recent move, but I give it anyway; I don't want my baby brother to die. I have moved to the most expensive city in the world. But I do not want my brother to die. My mom and cousin win guardianship. My brother survives.

I start to blame myself for his stroke. If he had lived with me, he would not have been on the streets. I start feeling guilty that I stayed in San Francisco instead of flying back to Arizona to help my mom with my brother. I remember when I still lived in Arizona, how

I took time out of my hectic schedule to help my mom. I was the good daughter and the good granddaughter – the person everyone called for financial support, technical support, legal support, and everything in-between. And I was exhausted with high blood pressure, a super-fast heart rate, anxiety, anemia, and prediabetes.

Had I stayed in Arizona or even returned during this time of tribulation, I would have been at the mercy of their needs.

I am so busy moving and starting a new job that it slips my mind just how much time and energy I spent helping everyone else. Now that I have a chance to breathe and relax, I realize how much weight is off my shoulders. Now I leave it in the hands of God.

17

New Beginnings

Therefore, if any man be in Christ, he is a new creature: old things are passed away; behold, all things are become new. (2 Corinthians 5:17)

I see that one of my favorite bands is performing at a local bar, and the DJ is performing, too. It will be nice to see everyone, or so I think. I arrive with a friend and notice a ring on the DJ's finger; he is married, and his statuesque wife is standing next to him behind the DJ booth. They look good together. He waves hello, but I ignore him; I am too shocked. But wait. His girlfriend is on the other side of the club, and his wife is oblivious to it all. The girlfriend is even more beautiful than his wife. His girlfriend appears to be having a meltdown in the middle of the dancefloor. While the DJ tries to calm down his girlfriend, his wife dances in place at the DJ booth, none the wiser. I feel bad for both women. The girlfriend eventually storms out of the club. I feel your pain, girl. He is the George Clooney of San Francisco. He's not ready to be faithful to one woman. His friend, the guitarist, sends me a private Facebook message a few weeks later.

"Happy Friday! I'm at Milk Bar tonight. It is going to be a funk party. Hope to see you there!"

The Holy Spirit tells me this is more than an invite to a gig. I learned my lesson last time from Twofer. Contrary to Snoop Dogg's "Ain't No Fun (If the Homies Can't Have None)", I will not date the DJ's friend, so I decline his invitation with a compliment.

"I enjoy your music, but I am not interested in receiving invites from [DJ's] gig mates/friends given the history I have with him. Regardless of your intentions, you know that I dated him briefly, and now that he's married, I find it disrespectful that you're inviting me to your show."

"Thanks for bringing this to my attention. No disrespect of any sort intended. I was not aware that [DJ] was married until I got this message from you. [DJ] never mentioned it to me. We see each other only rarely these days, and I only invited him to this event because he showed up at our Street party. And there, when he showed up, I thought that was his girlfriend, not his wife.

Anyway, thanks again for letting me know – I certainly would never knowingly disrespect you, and now that I am aware of your feelings, I will, of course, make sure they are respected going forward. Best to you!"

A friend asks me, "How do you know that the guitarist is not the one? What if he is the one, but you didn't give him a chance?"

It wouldn't be fair, not to me nor his friend. I would want to be with the DJ, not his friend. I can imagine going to a Thanksgiving celebration and seeing the DJ and staring longingly at him while I am there with his friend. What a depressing life.

THE DEVIL'S CONCUBINE

I see the guitarist every now and again at the grocery store and in Hayes Valley. But we never acknowledge each other.

A few months later, I buy a studio condo in a new and modern building with a tad bit of buyer's remorse. The floor-to-ceiling windows overlook a historic building with exceptional light exploding in my small space. My place reminds me of my college dorm life with house rules. What have I done? I have taken out a mortgage loan with interest to live inside an expensive room on the sixth floor. And there are a few downsides. Except for voting in Homeowners Association (HOA) elections, there is no power or control in a condo building as a homeowner. You cannot go to the rooftop and have a party till 3 a.m. Or paint the hallways red. Living here is unlike living in Arizona, where I don't need to negotiate parking fees at my residence. In my condo building, $100K buys you a parking spot, the city dictates the smoke alarm and fire sprinkler inspection schedule, and they don't care if you have to take a Zoom call when the alarms are blaring. The HOA hires someone to manage the general day-to-day activities of a multi-unit building. The HOA also has access to your unit and has the right to enter said unit within reason. After all, you are living in their house with many entities dictating rules. I am at the mercy of my neighbors adhering to the house rules, the HOA being a good steward of unit keys and the Covenants, Conditions, and Restrictions (CC&Rs), and the city of San Francisco providing reasonable notice to inspect my unit.

The upside of condo life in the city is everything I need is within walking distance, just 20 minutes away or less: malls, movies, grocery stores, restaurants, work, doctors, farmers market, and clubs. No yard to tend to, and I no longer worry about someone breaking into my place, with so many layers of security inherent in a modern building. The intruder would have to breach the building doors, the fob-enabled elevators, or the locked stairwell doors, and lastly, my unit door. In Arizona, I always lived in fear that someone would break into my house from any of the eight windows, the front door, the backdoor, the sliding glass door, or the garage door. However, I am at peace living in my condo. I feel safer here than I ever have in Arizona, partially due to the diversity in my hood; we are here, and we are Black. I never see a Confederate flag flying in San Francisco. It's nice living in a diverse city.

On the flip side, I think my place is so tiny. I feel that I should have purchased a bigger unit, but later, I learn to rejoice in buying the most affordable condo in the most expensive city in the United States. I am paying for peace of mind, proximity to necessities, and entertainment.

I appreciate my little haven, but is it a gift from God? He does not add sorrow to blessings. One will never know. One thing that is for sure is His grace helps me power through. I can hear my neighbors urinating in their bathroom on the other side of the shared wall. I can hear the shenanigans happening on the ground floor through my 6th floor vents. As a test, the HOA installs a silencer to mitigate the noise in another unit. But I will need to pay half the cost when they install it in my unit. Mosquitoes find their way into my place and sometimes bite me when I'm fast asleep, but I have recently added another ingredient to my homemade face cleanser that repels them. I ask

THE DEVIL'S CONCUBINE

God if it is OK to buy a place at a new condo development, to which he responds, "Only if you pay off your current mortgage loan first. You don't know the design deficiencies of the new building. New buildings have many unknowns as you very well know. It may be worse than mosquitoes."

OK. I'll stay put for now.

I was ready to sign on the dotted line when I wrote the love letter to San Francisco many moons ago, so I should not complain now.

A short-term rental agency manages the unit below me; it is different than the "dead body" building agency. The company furnishes the condo complete with a queen size bed, in-unit washer/dryer, and everything in-between. The unit even has high-speed internet and cable TV for a hefty fee. A woman moves in for a few months. She is quiet except for Sunday mornings when she turns on the TV at the highest volume and watches worship service. The people on the TV are hollering, screaming, and singing about Jesus. I roll my eyes and think to myself, Lady, your TV is too loud for a quiet Sunday morning, and I do not want to hear about Jesus right now. Little do I know that Jesus has other plans for me.

Exploring my new surroundings, I go to a restaurant where, to my surprise, I see the DJ working as a waiter. We exchange hugs, and I congratulate him on getting married. He looks happy.

One day as I walk home from work, I see the realtor – Apollonia's friend. It is an awkward exchange. San Francisco is the largest, smallest city you will ever live in because you always run into people from your past.

"I wish you could have gotten the commission from the condo I just bought. It is too bad Apollonia didn't want me to work with you." He tells me he likes my dress, and we go our separate ways. I never see him again.

I used to judge Audrey, Apollonia, Red, and Jolene/Celestine's ways of living and curse the SF men who hurt me until I realized that we are all the same – we are all sinners. The women of loose morals and no discretion attracting men who like strange women, as described in the scriptures – it is the allure and embodiment of the Jezebel spirit.

18

JESUS

But if from thence thou shalt seek the LORD thy God, thou shalt find him, if thou seek him with all thy heart and with all thy soul. (Deuteronomy 4:29)

I am on the second leg of the journey to a destination wedding in the Dominican Republic, on a three-hour flight, when I have a revelation about hell. I'm so thirsty, but I also want to avoid having to go to the restroom; I am in the middle seat and don't want the hassle of waking the guy in the aisle seat to go to the tiny lavatory in the back of the plane. So, I sit there the entire flight parched. My throat is so dry I start to wonder if this is the kind of thirst you feel in hell. "No, it will be much worse," says the Holy Spirit, "and it will be for an eternity."

I return home from the wedding. And lo and behold, I find God on YouTube. I see video recommendations about God, getting saved, death, and experiences on the other side before resuscitation. I can't brush it off as a coincidence. The videos keep popping up. I watch a video about a woman who briefly dies after being involved in a bus accident. She remembers going to hell; it was so hot, so much fire. The way she describes the fire reminds me of a high-speed car chase that ends in a fiery crash. Instead of

67

the driver dying instantly, he or she remains fully conscious, burning in the inferno in excruciating pain forever. She cries out to God and asks, "Why am I in hell?" She pleads with God because she does not understand what went wrong. She is a devout Catholic and always thought her resting place would be in Heaven. God tells her she did not forgive her mother. She has some festering resentment towards her mother, and she had to die to understand her sin of unforgiveness.

Many people are in hell now, hoping for a drop of water, a second chance, and an opportunity to warn their brothers on earth that hell is real, as the Rich Man pleads in Luke 16:19-31. Instead of receiving mercy, the Rich Man hears, "If they hear not Moses and the prophets, neither will they be persuaded, though one rose from the dead." The Rich Man is forever tormented in hell, remembering the days when he could have gotten saved.

This video resonates with me, and it also scares me. I have a lot of resentment and unforgiveness in my heart towards my dad. God sent his only son Jesus to die on the cross for our sins. If Jesus can forgive the men who crucified him on the cross, I should be able to forgive those who merely neglect and mistreat me (Luke 23:34). A few days later, I send my dad a text and tell him I want to move on from the past and forgive him for everything he has done to me. I also send a text to my favorite cousin and tell her the same. Because I'm human, I will probably never *forget* what they did, but I will not let my resentment for them block my salvation to be with the Lord in Heaven. Plus, it is so much easier to live life when you are not fixated on the past. You can't change the past. There

68

are some things I wish I did not have to live through, but without these tribulations, I wouldn't be the happy and successful person I am today. Growing pains turned into learning how to love. I'll let God judge those who've wronged me and those who have wronged those I love. I cannot compete with the vengeance of my Creator; He created everything, and His vengeance will be great. Greater than anything a man can do as His creation.

My late grandma couldn't convince me to change my ways. Neither could the therapist, but Jesus could, and He did it through YouTube. He came to me on my level. Why wouldn't He?

19

Rebirth

And fear not them which kill the body, but are not able to kill the soul; but rather fear him that is able to destroy both soul and body in hell. (Matthew 10:28)

I start dating a man who seems harmless. He lives in the neighborhood and is a strong, stocky man with broad shoulders – once used to carry a bookshelf down the street, I hear. He has a deep voice and is different than any man I've ever met. He is a man of few words, the silent type with a combination of rugged, action-packed leading man qualities like Clint Eastwood in *The Good, The Bad and The Ugly*, Ryan Gosling in *Drive*, and Liam Neeson in *Taken*. He reminds me of my papa, who used to carry a gun in his boot. One day, I tell him I don't feel comfortable walking down the street because the men harass and catcall me. He says he doesn't have that problem and that he could accompany me on my walks. Those walks turn into dates and then into a relationship. During our walks, no one harasses me, but they start harassing him ironically enough, mostly asking for money. He tells me, "If there ever comes a time when we are in a life or death situation, I want you to run for your life until you are safe. Don't worry about me. I will fight for your honor." His words strike me to my core and make me emotional the rest of the day. But there is a huge, flaming, red hot flag – he is more than 10 years my junior – and I ignore it.

Seven months later, he proposes, but he doesn't buy me an engagement ring. He says we'll pick it out together, but in the meantime, we can draft the prenuptial agreement.

"Do you want a prenuptial agreement?"

"Yes, what's yours is yours; what's mine…is mine," he says.

I accept the proposal, but the Holy Spirit tells me to wait and not go to the courthouse just yet. I would learn soon that my salvation was more important, and marrying him would jeopardize it further.

One day I break down in tears in front of my boyfriend. "I saw a man die today. He didn't know he was going to die when he got on his skateboard. But when I heard the sound of his skull hit the pavement, when he fell off his skateboard on Market Street, I knew he probably took his last breath. I didn't want to wait for confirmation. I am afraid. I'd never seen so much death till I moved here. Everywhere I turn. I see people overdosing outside my window. I see their faces turn blue – no pulse. They take a hit of fentanyl, crack cocaine, heroin, meth, or something else, and they're gone. Their bodies lie stiff on the ground: some dressed up; some dressed down; some come through on their lunch break; some come through with their suitcases in tow. The paramedics can revive some with Narcan, but others die. What if they died without being saved? I want to be saved when I die. There are so many earthquakes here. What if the big one comes and I'm not ready? I'm scared. I'm afraid I'm going to

71

die without being saved," I cry out while tears stream down my cheeks.

"It is OK. I will baptize you now, and if something happens to you, you will be saved and go to Heaven."

"But how does that even count? You're not a pastor."

"Where I'm from, religion is a part of education. Everyone studied the Bible from elementary through high school. I've read it cover to cover, too many times to count. I will baptize you."

"OK."

He looks up the words to use to baptize someone online. We do not use water, nor does he dip me in a body of water. He speaks words to me.

"Repent and ask God for forgiveness for all your sins." So, I do, under my breath.

"Lord, please forgive me for the abortions. Forgive me for being a horrible wife. Forgive me for using profanity. Forgive me for fornicating. Forgive me for being a bad granddaughter. Forgive me for not honoring my parents. Forgive me for being a bad friend. Forgive me for lying. Forgive me for all my trespasses and all of my sins of ignorance." (The list is too long for this book.)

I feel better the next day, but the Lord isn't satisfied. In the middle of a deep sleep, the Lord wakes me up and says, "Get baptized." Later that day, I call a local church and leave a voicemail. I found the church on Facebook four years ago, and it is still in my bookmarks. A woman calls back a few days later. I tell her I want to get baptized. She tells me the church has a Night Watch Service on New Year's Eve at 10 p.m., and I can get baptized then by the pastor. She verifies my contact information and tells me the pastor will call me back.

The pastor calls back a week later. He asks a few questions; I ask a few questions. He tells me that it counts that my boyfriend baptized me. I confirm with him that I'll be at the church before 10 p.m. on 12/31.

I tell a colleague about how I'm getting baptized in a few weeks.

He says, "Aren't you worried about losing your boyfriend? He is a good guy."

"If I lose him because of Jesus, he is not the man for me."

I get baptized on New Year's Eve. The water is so cold. Icy cold. So frigid that I have to catch my breath before I can utter a word. I am happy to be saved.

I return to the same church a few days later with my boyfriend for the 11:30 a.m. Sunday worship, where the doubting begins. A woman at the church says that she didn't think she'd ever see me again after my baptism.

That day will also be the last time my boyfriend steps inside the church. In the following weeks, I take a Lyft to church every Sunday, and he meets me outside the church to walk me home. He thinks it is just a joke, a fad, that I will revert to my old sinful ways. But my boyfriend is wrong, and the lady at the church is wrong. God has a call on my life, and no one can change it.

20

Bible

Heaven and earth shall pass way, but my words shall not pass away. (Matthew 24:35)

I purchase a Bible and start reading it, but don't understand it *initially*. I keep rereading the first few chapters in Genesis, but I can't finish the entire Book; it reads like a foreign language even though I am reading an English translation. The pastor always asks the congregation, do you have an illuminated Bible or a Bible? I have a Bible. The only illumination happening is with the reading light shining on it late at night. My boyfriend suggests I purchase a children's Bible. I had a children's Bible at one time that my grandma bought me decades ago, but I sold it on Etsy.

Then things with my boyfriend take a turn for the worse, and in less than two months, I break up with him.

He starts to speak out against the Lord. He thinks he can defeat God. To be sure he isn't joking, I ask him at different times. He says on three separate occasions that he will fight God on Judgment Day and win the battle with the artificial intelligence army he creates. He no longer reminds me of Papa.

Then he becomes a threat to others. He is aggressive with strangers, unprovoked – men and women. He deliberately walks into a man talking on his cell phone because "he was in the way". He practically dislodges a woman's shoulder as they pass each other on the sidewalk because "she is taking up more than her share of the sidewalk." He collides with her so hard that she grabs her shoulder and gasps.

"What is wrong with you? You shouldn't do that to a woman; that is assault! I bet you won't try that with a drug dealer in the Tenderloin, will you?"

He has nothing to say.

Then he tries to destroy my self-esteem. He doesn't hesitate to tell me I am neither a queen nor a princess. He says I have too much confidence and need to tone it down. He also tells me it is a chore for him to keep me happy. He reminds me all the time about all the good things he does for me. He wants me to praise him every day and wants to remind me of all the wrongs I do to him. He admits that he only has peace when he's walking alone because when I'm with him, the men always ask for money.

Then he wants me to rebel against the Lord. He tells me that fornication is not in the Ten Commandments and that it is stupid to abstain from sex until marriage. He says, "If you want to follow His commandments, go to church every Sunday and ask for forgiveness after sex." He insists if it is not a part of the Ten Commandments, it is not a sin. He says show him where in the Bible it is a part of the Ten Commandments. I know there are many commandments in the Bible, but not explicit commandments that are a part of the ten. Here are examples, you evil man of apostasy[3], which I'm sure

---

[3] Apostasy is total abandonment of the Christian faith; or refusing to continue to

you are fully aware of, but because you are of the adversary, you seek to confuse me:

Example #1

For out of the heart proceed evil thoughts, murders, adulteries, fornications, thefts, false witness, blasphemies:

These are *the things* which defile a man: but to eat with unwashen hands defileth not a man. (Matthew 15:19-20)

Example #2

For from within, out of the heart of men, proceed evil thoughts, adulteries, fornications, murders,

thefts, covetousness, wickedness, deceit, lasciviousness[4], an evil eye, blasphemy, pride,

foolishness:

All these evil things come from within, and defile the man. (Mark 7:21-23)

Example #3

Now the works of the flesh are manifest, which are *these*: Adultery, fornication, uncleanness, lasciviousness. (Galatians 5:19)

Evil man of apostasy, fornication serves Lucifer, death, and an eternity in hell, and I want an eternity with my Heavenly Father.

Then he uses my past against me. He is upset that I won't do to him what I had done to men before him. I am offended.

"You want me to revert to an insecure, demoralized woman so you can have your way sexually with me? I will not provoke the Lord. I will not revert to the way I used to live, when I was unlearned and of the flesh,

---

follow the Christian faith.
[4] Lasciviousness is giving into or expressing sexual desire or lust.

so that you can defile me at your leisure. Do you know how much work, counseling, and time I spent getting to where I am now, to a peaceful and healthy state?"

"Why should I have to suffer because you feel better about yourself now?"

"No. I feel secure in my skin and am no longer afraid now that I am baptized. Now I only fear God."

"That's blasphemy to fear God," he says.

"I rebuke you in the name of Jesus Christ. The devil is a liar!"

Then he attempts to make me feel guilty about how much money he spends on me. "I spent over $6,000 on this relationship so far. I added up all the money I spent on expensive dates, traveling, food delivery, and miscellaneous stuff."

"And? You want me to pay you back? Because I won't. Did you tell the women before me to pay you back? Did you keep a running tally and tell them how much you spent? No? I didn't think so."

Then he destroys my property, but I can't prove it. One day I attend my company's holiday party. He doesn't want to go. While at the party, my phone dies, or at least that's what I think initially. It turns out that my phone gets erased; all the images, text messages, contacts – gone. I think he erased my phone out of spite because I still went to the party without him. He has the technical aptitude to do it. And if anyone could do it, it is him. And of all the cell phones I have owned, not one has had its data erased. I should have known this could happen when he insisted that I purchase the same phone make and model from Best Buy that he had purchased a few months earlier. I leave the party early; I don't feel comfortable staying there without having the means to call for help in a city like San

Francisco. So, I have someone at the party call me a Lyft, and I go home just as the party is getting started. I ask him to help retrieve my phone data, but he can't.

Then he tries to put me on ice. He comes over and tells me he needs some time to think about what he wants to do with his life. He needs a break from our relationship, in other words. He doesn't know if I'm the woman for him. He says, "If a woman wants to come and sit on my dick, I will let her."

This is the last time he sets foot in my place. The next day he invites me to come over, but instead, I break up with him over the phone. The pandemic hits, San Francisco goes into lockdown, and the church closes its doors.

I am alone again. No boyfriend, living in a tiny studio again, but this time it is happening during a pandemic, and I am happy, not broken. I have my Bible, and I am studying the Word on Zoom six times a week. My favorites are Bible study, Sunday school, and Bible review. I feel safe amid a pandemic. Had it not been for the love of God in my life, I would have stayed with the man of apostasy despite the red flags, as I did in previous relationships before He saved my life. But the old Dawn died and is reborn in the Word of God. Only God.

21

Illuminated Bible

Blessed is he that readeth, and they that hear the words of this prophecy, and keep those things which are written therein: for the time is at hand. (Revelation 1:3)

As soon as I turn my back on the man of apostasy, my Bible becomes an illuminated Bible. Living in willful sin was blocking my understanding of the Word. My reading comprehension becomes clear. God knows my questions before I ask them verbally and directs me to the answers. Sometimes, someone else speaking on a different topic gives me closure to a question I've had for some time without my saying a word. The Bible is man's user manual for himself. I don't need to adhere to the latest fad diet when I have the Bible to tell me what food to eat. From frenemies to finances, the Bible is my reference book for all matters. He and His Word are divine, glorious, and on time.

My illuminated Bible begins to remove doubts about our Lord and Savior. I doubted like the disciples. How is it possible for Jesus to be resurrected? He dies on the cross but rises three days later? I cannot wrap my brain around it until I read the convincing proof that He did rise, and He will return. The most compelling evidence, in my opinion, is the account of Mary Magdalene. She is at the cross before His

79

crucifixion, during His crucifixion, and after His crucifixion. (The disciples run away out of fear.) Mary Magdalene is one of the first people our Lord and Savior speaks to the day He rises in John 20:11-18. The disciples do not believe Jesus when he foretells the resurrection, nor Mary Magdalene when she confirms the resurrection. The disciples do not believe He has risen until He appears before them in John 20:19-31. Jesus tells them to preach the Word to everyone so that they will be ready for His return. Will you believe today that He will return before it is too late for your salvation?

22

Discernment

Regard not them that have familiar spirits, neither seek after
wizards, to be defiled by them: I am the LORD your God.
(Leviticus 19:31)

Reading the Bible makes it easier to discern the
voice of God versus the voice of evil. Know the
difference. If it is evil, it is not of God; it is of the
adversary. God is real, and so is Satan. Even Satan
knows God is real, and demons tremble before Him,
according to James 2:19. Just like there are churches to
worship God, there are Freemason lodges that worship
Satan, and they are in every town in the United States.

Freemasons worship Satan, also referred to as
Lucifer, according to the Freemasonry founder Albert
Pike, who said, "The true and pure philosophical
religion is the belief in Lucifer, the equal of Adonai, but
Lucifer, god of light and god of good, is struggling for
humanity against Adonai, the god of darkness and evil"
(A.C. De La Rive, La Femme et L'enfant dans La
Franc-Maconnerie Universelle, pgs. 588-89). Look
closely for the signs, hand gestures, and specific attire.
The architect's compass with or without the all-seeing
eye is their logo. They have several handshakes and
hand placements, and they wear aprons and gloves.
Look around you, and you will see that many police

departments, doctors, musicians, rappers, and actors are Freemasons. Do they take orders from the top 33° Sovereign Grand Inspector General Freemasons to carry out atrocities for Lucifer?

Lucifer has infiltrated the state police. Assassinating Black and Brown men has been normalized. "If he's White, save his life. If he's Brown or Black, pop a cap." My Brown and Black brothers are dying at the hands of the law. Tamir Rice, Michael Brown, Eric Garner, Philando Castile, George Floyd, Daunte Wright, Freddie Gray, Manuel Ellis, Antonio Valenzuela, and Adam Toledo are gone.

Lucifer has infiltrated our hospitals. Maiming, killing, misdiagnosing, and mistreating Black and Brown people have been normalized. A whistleblower exposed a physician's assistant in Texas with damning evidence rife with racism and inhumane treatment of people of color requiring medical attention.

Lucifer has infiltrated music. Many rappers and rock musicians admit to selling their souls to the devil. I once saw a broadcast of a rapper performing on stage, telling his audience, "You are going to hell with me." Another rapper, married to a beautiful and famous artist, used backmasking[5] on one of his albums speaking against Jesus. The same rapper was filmed dancing and chanting with a high-ranking witch who filmed a spirit cooking ritual. This rapper wears clothing that reads, "Do what thou wilt," which goes against the Bible. Another rapper, who partnered with a shoe company to make Satan shoes containing a drop of blood in the soles, made a music video performing

---

[5] Backmasking is deliberately recording a message that can only be understood when it is played backwards.

illicit acts with Satan. Many musicians use the 666 hand gesture, sometimes over the eye. It's the mark of the beast, not Jesus, according to Revelation 13.

Hand photo created by jcomp-www.freepik.com

Lucifer has infiltrated television. Some TV talking heads push their antichrist and confusion agendas to the masses. A famous talk show host says that she doesn't want to follow a jealous God. And there is more than one way to salvation. No, there is only one way to salvation, and that way is through Jesus Christ, according to John 14. Other shows like *Lucifer* distort Bible truths and portray Satan as good to confuse the masses. In an episode of *Legends of Tomorrow,* the Satanist Aleister Crowley is glorified. The episode pokes fun at teaching children witchcraft. Witchcraft is neither fun nor funny.

Lucifer has infiltrated the movies. Some in the film industry curse and mock our Lord. God's name is cursed and used in vain in too many movies to list. Some movies mock the Word. In *Twilight: New Moon,* Bella sees Edward in the wilderness with beautiful glowing skin like the sun, as if he were transfigured like Jesus on the mountaintop in Matthew 17. In *The*

Village, the townspeople paint the doors red to mock the Passover in Exodus 13.

Lucifer has infiltrated video games. In the video game *The Legend of Zelda*, there are burning bushes throughout the scenes to mock the burning bush before Moses when God spoke to him in Exodus 3.

If you are not for God, you are with Lucifer. Lucifer's evil works will continue to infiltrate our lives through the law, healthcare, and entertainment, and he *will* torment you in hell for eternity. I'm afraid that unsuspecting Christians are not aware that following these people and their methods could jeopardize their salvation. How do you know someone is working for the adversary? Discernment. Will you use discernment to identify evil, turn away from evil, and repent? The end *is* near.

23

Spiritual Warfare

Be sober, be vigilant; because your adversary the devil, as a roaring lion, walketh about, seeking whom he may devour (1 Peter 5:8)

In the months following my breakup, spiritual warfare is at its height. I have double dreams of being intimate with people I know. The devil is tempting me with fornication, adultery, and evil thoughts. I dream about sleeping with coworkers, someone's husband, a woman, and a man of the cloth. The devil is trying me, but I know what he is doing. I rebuke him in the name of Jesus Christ. The dreams don't completely stop, but they become fewer and far between.

The devil reminds me of my trespasses. Why do you remind me of those things for which God has already forgiven? I rebuke you, Satan.

I also keep running into the man of apostasy on weekends and weekdays, several times a month. It never ends. I have to change the time of day I step outside my front door to run errands. I remember he is most active at night, so I switch from late afternoons and evenings to early mornings to run basic errands and finally stop running into him so much.

24

God's Favor

For whoso findeth me findeth life, and shall obtain favour of the LORD. (Proverbs 8:35)

I start seeing more favor in my life after my rebirth. Before getting saved, I was complacent at the same bank for almost 15 years. God's favor starts to manifest – a new job with a 12% salary increase plus stock shares. The position calls for moving a manual, Excel-driven process to an automated process housed in a database to extract data from multiple systems, transform the data, and load the data (ETL) into an organized report-ready format. I panic. I haven't built a warehouse before or even an ETL process. I pray about it. In four months, I accomplish what multiple people and groups could not do in years. In four more months, the system is production-ready. If not for God, I would not have been able to do it. He put people in my life who would help me; the man of apostasy helped me practice for the job interview, and the people on the job helped me get to the finish line.

Senior management in the company is so happy with my work that they approve a merit increase during the pandemic when the company has to lay off 10% of its workforce and cut salaries by 10%. HR says not only do I get a merit increase effective immediately, but I will also get another increase once HR fully restores salaries to pre-pandemic levels. When I receive my W2 for my first full year working at this new company, I realize my salary has increased by 25%.

God's favor has others asking, "Is this something Dawn can do?" With new projects on the horizon, my name comes up more frequently in conversations, and people want my help. The work is so diverse and rich in complexity I feel my brain absorbing the new skills like a sponge, preparing me for what the Lord has in store for me.

25

The Voice and Hand of God

My sheep hear my voice, and I know them, and they follow me:
And I give unto them eternal life; and they shall never perish,
neither shall any man pluck them out of my hand.
(John 10:27-28)

God regularly speaks to me: in dreams, while awake, while alone, and while surrounded by a sea of people walking down the streets. When the pandemic hits, I don't know whether to sell my condo and move back to Arizona, save money, or pay off debt. As I awake one morning, He tells me to save my money. Recently, He tells me to "cross the street" as I am walking to Trader Joe's; a woman gets assaulted on the same path I would have taken shortly after. I used to feel so inconvenienced in the morning that I had to take an extra step and put in my contact lenses, to read my email without having my face close to the laptop screen. Immediately, I hear, "At least you still have sight." I never complain again. It is fascinating how He communicates with me, and I am grateful that I recognize His voice.

God wakes me up in the middle of the night to give me the title of this book. I procrastinate a bit till He tells me to start writing for a least an hour a day. I do this till one day, a Saturday, His words keep downloading into my mind, to my fingertips, to the keyboard, and I write all day long from 8 a.m. to 10 p.m. When I have questions about the content, He answers me during Sunday school, while studying the Word, and even while I am watching YouTube videos. He brings suppressed memories to the forefront of my remembrance so that I can share my journey to follow Him.

Many people call it intuition, an instinct, or a hunch, but it is the Holy Spirit. Jesus promised us that he would not leave us on earth alone without guidance before He died on the cross. In His stead, God sent the Holy Spirit as an intercessor, our mediator, our guardian, our protector, and the Holy Spirit is that something, that voice you refer to when you tell a story that starts with the words, "And something told me to XYZ."

During the pandemic, I feel His wedge of protection. I am at ground zero of sin in all forms and on a larger scale. The lawlessness usually occurs within a few hundred feet of my building: death, burglary, murder, rape, robbery, assault, and gun battles. But I am protected by the blood of Jesus.

26

Rapture

Immediately after the tribulation of those days shall the sun be darkened, and the moon shall not give her light, and the stars shall fall from heaven, and the powers of the heavens shall be shaken:
And then shall appear the sign of Son of man in heaven: and then shall all the tribes of the earth mourn, and they shall see the Son of man coming in the clouds of heaven with power and great glory. (Matthew 24:29-30)

I wake up to a dark, orange sky. It is 8 a.m., and it is so dark outside my window that I have to turn on my lights to start the day. My first thought is, did I miss the Rapture? Did Jesus return and leave me here? Please, God, I hope I didn't miss it.

Then shall two be in the field; the one shall be taken, and the other left.
Two women shall be grinding at the mill; the one shall be taken, and the other left.
Watch therefore: for ye know not what hour your Lord doth come. (Matthew 24:40-42)

It wasn't the Rapture. It was California's wildfire smoke blocking the sun's beautiful rays. I am relieved to know I am saved and am ready for Jesus to return. I want to be with my Lord and Savior in Heaven.

27

Church

For God is not the author of confusion, but of peace, as in all churches of the saints. (1 Corinthians 14:33)

As a newbie, being a church member can be your rock, but I believe God led me to this particular church to strengthen its foundation. From what I can tell, its foundation is sand.

I ask a friend before the pandemic hits, "How do I find a good church?"

"You have to go and visit in person," he says. "You'll know if it is the right church for you."

I am reluctant to join the first church I visit. I have many questions about what it means to be a church member and receive vague answers. The youth director introduces herself to me. I tell her I'm too old to be in the youth ministry.

"You're not older than I am, are you? I'm 40."

"Yes, I'm over 40 – too old to be in the youth ministry," I say.

"That is OK. We'll claim you."

"What does it entail to be a member of the church?"

"Nothing," she says.

A few weeks later, and despite my age, the youth director tells me she will give me the script for my role in a play happening next Sunday during morning worship.

Excuse me? I did not commit to participating in a play at church in front of the congregation, I thought to myself. The audacity of not asking me first if I am available to do it and then assuming that I will do it because you asked me to do it – it angers me. I tell her I cannot participate, and she looks at me in disbelief. Apparently, as a church member, you are supposed to be obedient to the senior members.

I am even more reluctant to join still. Every week, the pastor routinely asks if anyone wants to become a member. Like clockwork and like the dog in Pavlov's experiment that salivates every time it hears the bell, one lady standing in the pews two rows in front of me slowly turns her neck around to look at me as if she is telepathically telling me to join. Stop looking at me, lady.

One day during Sunday service, I hear trap music coming from the pulpit. Trap music is a sub-genre of hip-hop music about illegal activities happening in drug/trap houses. Is the devil in this church? I don't know any God-fearing churches listening to rap, trap, or hip-hop music *inside* the church. It could have been someone's ringtone because it takes a minute to stop. You cannot listen to that type of music when you serve Jesus. You cannot partake in both worlds; you pick a side, which means do not listen to music about doing illegal activities if you are for the Lord.

After the lockdown, the pastor conducts church services online. To my surprise, he adds me as a church member despite not speaking to me first. It becomes a feeding frenzy – ladies, young and old, from the church calling incessantly, asking for my participation in church services.

"Can you provide a testimony? Can you read scripture? Can you sing?"

"No. No. No."

I send the pastor an email.

"Pastor, the church is out of order. No one told me as a new member that I would be required to participate in any church service, nor that someone would publish my phone number in the church directory. I am here to learn. God did not tell me to give my testimony on Facebook Live. I have a demanding job that I'd very much like to keep, a family to attend to, and I need to avoid burnout. So, I am unwilling and unable to participate in any church service, in any capacity."

"OK. I will ask the ladies not to call you."

"Thank you."

But it doesn't end there. The pastor wants to elevate me to a teacher within three months of joining his church. I tell him and everyone listening in on Zoom, "I need to be a good steward of the Word. I am not ready to teach the congregation when I am illiterate in the Word of God."

"We're here to guide you," he says. "Try it. You can call me if you have any questions about the lesson."

"My answer is still the same. I will let you know when I'm ready. I'm not ready now."

The pastor asks the members to buy the book *Holy Spirit Power* by Charles Spurgeon. Something leads me to an article that indicates this author could send me into damnation, but I don't completely understand why until much later. I dismiss the warning and continue attending because I want to learn the Word.

THE DEVIL'S CONCUBINE

I send him a few links to help our church broadcast on YouTube, which is his cue to announce to the congregation, without discussing with me first, that I have accepted a position on the church technical team.

I send him a text immediately, and he calls.

"Pastor, I am here to learn the Word. If I'm distracted by disruptive noises on Zoom *and* trying to determine who I should mute, I may miss an important message. I do not want to miss anything. Being a Zoom administrator will be a hindrance to my learning journey."

"OK, First Lady, and I appreciate your maturity in this matter."

"Good. Thank you."

A few months into the pandemic, he says to me on Zoom before the congregation, "Turn on your camera. I need to see your face.

"No. I am on Zoom all day long at work. I am not turning on my camera."

Seeing my face on Zoom has nothing to do with my salvation. Why are you calling me out and no one else?

The requests become ridiculous, almost willfully ignorant.

"I want volunteers to accompany me in the Tenderloin and wash the feet of the homeless."

The congregation is silent, and no one volunteers. A week later, one person volunteers, but the pastor expects more participation and pierces our hearts with guilt. Oh really, pastor? We are in the middle of a pandemic. There are many services to provide for the homeless, and foot washing is not one of them. Some of the homeless are sick, scared, hungry, and disturbed. They could stab us, spit on us, spread or be exposed to COVID, or worse. How about casting out demons first as Jesus did? The homeless have a hierarchy of needs, and foot washing seems to be at the bottom.

I send him an email later that day asking if he can have an infectious disease expert speak to the congregation about protecting ourselves when feet-washing during a pandemic. He never mentions feet-washing again. He says he'll invite an infectious disease expert to talk to us and teach us how to be safe, but no one ever speaks to the congregation.

But there is more.

"Dawn, can you type the summary of the lesson in the Zoom group chat?"

"No, Pastor, I cannot take personal notes and write in the group chat at the same time."

And later, "Dawn, I'm going to promote you to co-host for Zoom. You don't have to do anything. I want to be sure if I accidentally lose my connection, the meeting will not disconnect everyone." Didn't I tell you I do not have the throughput to serve in any capacity in the church while I'm learning the Word of God? What part of "no" do you not understand?

One of the church missionaries defies the pastor's request to not call on me for participation. She asks me to participate on Zoom again. "Sister Dawn, can you read the prayer from our Sunday school book?"

No. I ignore the request and keep my microphone on mute. What part of my camera is off, with a muted microphone tells you I want to read during Bible study early on Sunday morning? I solve Bible-based crossword puzzles, participate in lively discussions about what we've read in the Bible, study at home, and ask questions during Bible study and Bible review. I will keep my session on mute with my camera off. I will unmute when I'm ready to speak.

THE DEVIL'S CONCUBINE

It gets creepy to the point where I consider leaving the church. I join a church Zoom call early, and the pastor and I are the only ones connected.

"Dawn, please turn on your camera. I haven't seen you in over a year."

I stall. Someone else joins.

He says, "Stay on at the end, and you can turn on your camera then."

"OK."

The Zoom call nears an end. I leave the meeting. Pastor calls me on my cell phone after 8 p.m. and asks me to join Zoom again. He laughs, but I don't think it is funny.

"No, that would be awkward for me to join Zoom with the two of us. Have your wife call me, and I'll do a FaceTime with her. But not tonight; it is too late."

"OK, I'll let First Lady know to call you and check on you." Why does anyone need to check on me if you see my name on every Zoom call and you hear me speaking a couple of times a week?

First Lady never calls. Is Pastor full of ill intentions?

I ask the Lord, why is the pastor out of line, demanding, and a bit of a dictator? Why does he cross the line and ask to see my face on Zoom and no one else's face? Why does it matter if my camera is off, but you can hear my voice? I have faithfully participated in all Zoom calls from the start of the pandemic. He asks me to turn on my camera, not others. I think it is disrespectful to his wife if he is only asking me. You will not see my face on Zoom. Seek the face of your wife. Better yet, seek the face of the Lord.

I cry out to the Lord, Should I find a new church? Should I tell his wife how he makes me uncomfortable, asking me to turn on my camera? Will the pastor lie

97

and say he is a good shepherd checking in personally with all the saints? Will he call me egocentric? Or, will he apologize and repent? Will I be the one to bring order, structure, and wise counsel to a church in trouble? Is the church in trouble? Or am I too sensitive? I am awaiting a response.

My prediction is accurate; I receive my answers one day after submitting this manuscript to my editor and again weeks later for good measure. The pastor justifies his behavior by quoting several passages from multiple Books of the Bible that describe the characteristics of a good pastor, including John 10 and several verses in Jeremiah 12 and 23: a good pastor checks on the sheep, including visiting them at their homes despite being in the middle of a pandemic, among other things. A member of the congregation asks a question, which mirrors my concern, "What should we do if the pastor is a bad shepherd?"

"Then, saints, you must pray for him," he says.

The church may have some issues, but the pastor does have a way of teaching the Word. It's dynamic, engaging, and I learn something new during each service. He is saving souls for the Lord. Many churches teach about prosperity alone, but not my pastor; he teaches about God, Jesus, the Holy Spirit, heaven, hell, Lucifer, fire, and brimstone. I cannot see going to another church right now, but there are other nuances beyond my immediate relationship with the congregation that require further discernment.

Some church members at the state and jurisdictional level currently serve in fraternities and sororities. According to my understanding of the Bible, any group that holds rituals in secret is against the Bible. You are not to take oaths, according to the Bible. Fraternities and sororities do both. Some fraternities and sororities even recite oaths to false gods with images of those false gods on their insignias like Athena, Thoth, Horus, Atlas, and the Sphinx to name a few. Built on a masonic foundation, their insignias also include masonic imagery. One cannot love God *and* serve false gods. Does the person at the top need a refresher in the doctrine to prevent the congregation from falling into condemnation?

I ask the pastor why leaders at the top aren't required to step down while living in willful sin.

"There are several branches of this church. While we report up through one branch, I can't control what happens at the top, but no one in my church is a member of a sorority nor a fraternity," he says. He continues, "Years ago, someone asked me to join a local Freemason lodge, but I declined." I am relieved to know that he denied partnering with a Luciferian doctrine. But it also makes me wonder how many Christian leaders have joined the occult, oblivious or not to the implications. And how many of those Freemason leaders shepherd the millions of members that belong to this church today? A member at the top is frequently photographed using a gesture in which he holds his hands before him in the shape of a diamond, which looks exactly like the Masonic symbol resembling the compass and square.

What's more disturbing is leadership at the top of my church is great friends with a megachurch leader who has troubling connections. This leader partners with the same antichrist TV talking head who foolishly believes there is more than one way to salvation. The megachurch leader should stop playing Patty Cake with salvation and tell the masses the truth! Right the wrongs propagating throughout the brethren. The salvation of the people is at hand, and as a teacher, one will be judged more harshly, according to James 3:1. God will hold one personally accountable for not telling the masses they are sinning, according to Ezekiel 3:18.

The breaking point for me is when I hear, during a Sunday school Facebook Live session, a pastor from a different branch referencing Charles Spurgeon. That name rings a bell. The Holy Spirit tried to tell me a year ago that Charles Spurgeon was a Freemason. I didn't want to believe that my church was teaching a Freemason's doctrine, but it's true. I do my research. Spurgeon's writings use masonic vocabulary and blaspheme the acts of God, Jesus, and the Holy Ghost by referring to them as *magic*. Magic is witchcraft; witchcraft is Lucifer. This entire congregation is in more trouble than I anticipated. The bad shepherds at the top explain some of the lost sheep at the bottom.

I ask the pastor via email, "Why is the church referencing Luciferian doctrine from Charles Spurgeon's teachings to preach to the congregation? Last year, when we read *Holy Spirit Power*, the Holy Spirit tried to tell me that Spurgeon was a deceiver, but I didn't want to believe our church would teach the word of a deceiver. Then last night during service online, it was brought to my attention when the Elder referenced Spurgeon's teachings. Further research indicates that Spurgeon's Freemason beliefs were reflected in his teachings. According to the Freemasons founder Albert Pike, Freemasons worship Lucifer as their god of light.

I know you said you turned down the request to join the Freemasons, which is a relief, but from my observation, I see signs of Freemasonry at the top. I know you said you don't have control over what happens at the top or at other branches. But I am still concerned about the salvation of members when teachings are not strictly those of our Lord and Savior Jesus Christ. It is our responsibility to tell people when they are sinning, and someone needs to alert the masses ASAP."

He's not ready to answer immediately. He needs time to pray and review Spurgeon's sermons (included in the email for reference) as he does not want to respond in haste. Fair enough.

A day after the email exchange, the pastor tells the congregation via Zoom that he awoke in the middle of the night to writing on the wall, but he couldn't read it. So, he starts praying. Is it God confirming my email to the pastor? The writing is on the wall. Will you believe it, Pastor? It scares me. If this is true, this is huge. What will the pastor do? What will I do if the pastor disagrees? If the pastor disagrees with me, I'll need to ask God for guidance.

The pastor responds three days later. He agrees. The sermons referring to the power of Jesus, God, and the Holy Spirit as magic are "incomprehensible". But he didn't use those sermons in any of *his* lessons. He says many highly educated church leaders consider Spurgeon to be a "Great Theologian". Yep, I'll need to ask God for guidance. The Holy Spirit gives me the information to include in a follow-up email. Our Sunday school material is full of vocabulary that could confuse a new Christian, considering it refers to Jesus as The One, as if it were written by Morpheus in *The Matrix*. The same text also calls Jesus Master of the Universe as if he is a cartoon character. Nowhere in the Bible is Jesus ever called The One. However, idolatrous religions call their false gods The One and Master of X. I find a Spurgeon sermon where he calls God a Freemason.[6] Blasphemy. God can never be a Freemason nor man. He is God. I will keep it simple and refer to God as Father, like Jesus.

Pastor responds to my email with urgency. He will send an official letter to the top of the congregation to determine who is writing their material. He alerts the church members on Zoom, too. He appreciates the level of maturity conveyed in the email. He also apologizes to the congregation for introducing this author to us and asks us to continue to be careful with the material we choose to read. I am overwhelmed with joy and relief. I thank him for his leadership and for being the vessel in my journey of finding truth in the Word.

Just as I am rejoicing in my renewed solidarity with the ecclesia[7], Pastor confounds me again; he thinks it's a good idea to demonstrate the idolatrous hand gesture, which looks like a triangle to reference Godhead in the Bible.

---

[6] Metropolitan Tabernacle Pulpit. (January 22, 1983). Abraham, A Pattern To Believers. Retrieved from: https://www.spurgeongems.org/sermon/chs2292.pdf
[7] Ecclesia is the Greek word for church.

THE DEVIL'S CONCUBINE

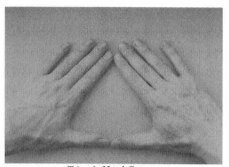

Triangle Hand Gesture

Some fraternities, sororities, freemasons, and Satanists also use the same hand gesture revering that which is not of God. Unless you are in the American Sign Language field, Christians should not make hand signs that could be mistaken for idolatry, in my opinion. I'll voice my concerns again to the pastor and hope for the best.

God, it's in your hands now. I'll let you worry about the church while I stay focused on the Word. Some of the branches on this tree are rotten, and only You can cut them down.

28

Full Circle

Remember ye not the former things, neither consider the things of old.
Behold, I will do a new thing; now it shall spring forth; shall ye not know it? I will even make a way in the wilderness, and rivers in the desert. (Isaiah 43:18-19)

I receive a letter that the city is building housing for the formerly homeless, and night construction will begin soon for approximately two months from 10 p.m. to 7 a.m., Sunday through Thursday. The noise will be considerably loud, with horns blaring every hour and bright lights illuminating the work. I inquire about renting a furnished unit. I find a cozy condo on the top floor in Hayes Valley a few blocks away from Patricia's Green, next to my favorite spots, Blue Bottle Coffee and Smitten Ice Cream. But I am turned off immediately when the property manager opens the front door to the building and the smell of cat urine overwhelms me.

I continue my search when I remember the short-term rental agency I used for my first summer stay in San Francisco. Great. It'll be a mini vacation. I can sleep at night. Plus, I can get away from the crazy antics of my beloved hood. On move-in day, everything goes as planned till I open the door of the unit. There are dead cockroaches on the kitchen floor and a dead bee on the floor between the bed and the open window. I have seen cockroaches before in San Francisco but not inside my house. I text the property manager, and she finds another unit in the same building. There are no bugs on the floor, but I notice that this is the same unit where the lady died of a heart attack, and SFFD asked if I could identify her body. This cute building will forever be known as the "dead body roach motel".

A few weeks later, the program manager for the homeless housing project tells me they are offering stipends for residents who may need to sleep elsewhere during the twilight work. This news has to be God's doing, and I will wait for Him to find a quiet place for me to sleep.

It turns out that God has already given me a quiet place to sleep – my condo. Night construction starts, and I have a $3,000 stipend in my pocket, but I take a chance and see how loud the noise will be outside my place before checking into the hotel I booked. The noise is so faint I sleep through the work that night and each night during the entire six-week process. Isn't God good?

29

Heaven

And I saw a new heaven and a new earth: for the first heaven and the first earth were passed away; and there was no more sea. (Revelation 21:1)

The Book of Revelation describes the new heaven and earth after He returns. No moon or sun, only the glory of God will provide light. The city streets are paved in gold, surrounded by walls of precious stones and 12 pearly gates.

Death, pain, suffering – no more. Those whose names are in the book of life will spend eternity with our Heavenly Father, Lord, and Savior Jesus Christ. Will your name be on the pages therein?

30

Transformation

And Jesus looking upon them saith, With men it is impossible, but not with God: for with God all things are possible. (Mark 10:27)

My life is now full of fervent prayer. I pray to Him daily, several times a day. I thank Him for waking me up in the morning and giving me the activity of my limbs. I pray my way out of every situation and before every battle. Problems at work, problems at home – nothing is too big for the Lord. I pray and leave it in His hands. I ask the Lord to speak through me to allow me to use His words to type and His words to write. I pray at night before I fall asleep with thanksgiving, grateful that He keeps me safe in the hustle and bustle of the city. I pray for my friends, family, strangers, enemies, and even those like the man of apostasy who used to know Him. To those close to me and who know the man of apostasy: please do not berate him. Instead, pray for him. God, thank you. What the devil meant for bad you turned into good. You used a non-believer as my protector until I could reach you. My ex brought me to Your house to get baptized. I was too afraid to go alone.

God, thank you for showering me with your grace to handle the roaring lions I face. They are loud and angry, but with prayer, their countenance[8] changes. And now they are gentle giants.

God, it took me a long time to find You. Thank you for being patient with me.

I am the intercessor for my family, and He has transformed us.

My brother transformed. From his death bed to a wheelchair, he is walking again with the help of a brace. He communicates now using complete sentences and can recall details and phone numbers for and about people and places in his life from decades ago. Only God could transform him. Only God.

My mom transformed. She now reads scriptures on forgiveness, how to release anger, and prays more using the new Bible she recently purchased. She talks to my brother about Jesus, too, and I rejoice in it. I love it when God uses me to reach others. Only God could transform her. Only God.

I transformed. From a non-believer to a worker for the Lord, I am reborn. I now spend my weekend studying the Word instead of going out. I write about Him in published works and speak about Him to anyone who will listen. He unstuck the tip of my tongue to speak His word, opened my ears to hear His voice, softened my heart to love Him, opened my eyes to see Him, and directed my feet to follow Him. I know Him. Only God could transform me. Only God.

---

[8] Countenance is the look or expression of the face.

31

Temptation

Blessed is the man that endureth temptation: for when he is tried, he shall receive the crown of life, which the Lord hath promised to them that love him. (James 1:12)

The temptation will never go away even when saved. Living by the Word makes it easier to resist. I find myself reminiscing about old times, listening to jazz at a lounge, getting notifications for bands I used to watch performing nearby. Even if I delete Facebook, temptations still abound. The devil's wiles cunningly alert me via phone app to the dangers around, coincidentally showing me a video of police activity at the hotel where the band I used to love performs. In the video, their music plays in the background. The temptation isn't necessarily the band; it's how the music makes me feel, bringing remembrance of untethered and unfettered wild adventures that took my focus away from God. Instead, he removes the worldly nature of my flesh, bringing focus to what He wants me to do next. Despite the temptation, with God, I will endure.

32

Wisdom

Who is a wise man and endued with knowledge among you? Let him shew out of a good conversation his works with meekness of wisdom. (James 3:13)

I learned a few key takeaways in my journey to find Jesus.

1. We are all sinners, *even* when saved. Only Jesus Christ is without sin, and he died on the cross for our sins.

2. God, Jesus, and Satan are real. With whom will you spend eternity? Please choose now and get ready. If you are reading these words, you have time to repent, get baptized, and accept Jesus as your Lord and Savior. (If you're already baptized, repent and ask Him for forgiveness.)

3. There is no such thing as a good witch or bad witch. A witch conjures spirits that are not of God.

4. God sees all sin the same. No sin is worse than the other. Fornication, cursing, murder, and lying are equal sins. So, sin no more.

5. Treating fornication as a sin helps protect you from *more* harm and from giving your body to a man who does not love you.

6. There is only one God. Place no other gods before Him.

7. Refer to the following word substitution matrix when reading the Bible to increase reading comprehension. Some of us don't use words like thou, thee, wilt, saith, or unto. The following matrix substitutes Bible words with plain English words.

Bible word	Plain English word
Nigh	Near
Peradventure	Perhaps
Tarry	Stay
Thee	You
Thou	You
Unto	To
Verily	With certainty
Ye	You
Any word that ends with ILT	Substitute LT with LL Wilt = will
Any word that ends with ITH	Substitute TH with D, e.g., saith = said
Any word that ends with LETH	Substitute ETH with ES or S, e.g., defileth = defiles calleth = calls
Any word that ends with NST	Substitute NST with N'T Canst = Can't
Any word that ends with OTH	Substitute TH with ES, e.g., doth = does
Any word that ends with KETH	Substitute KETH with KS Walketh = walks

8. Identify whether or not a man is your husband
    early in the courtship; recognize red flags early.
    Out of all the men from my past, only one
    asked for my hand in marriage, married me, and
    loved me like God loves the church. Some
    men will only propose and not go to the altar.
    The man of apostasy asked me to marry him,
    but we didn't go to the altar. Some men will go
    to the altar but not love their wives like God
    loves the church. Until a man does all three, he
    is a lesson learned. I compiled a more thorough
    list of lessons learned to help you qualify a man
    quickly with the Lessons Learned Man Matrix.

Lessons Learned Man Matrix

Lesson Learned	Description	Why Lesson Learned?
1	Asks for threesomes	Does not want you Does not respect you
2	Offers you drugs	Hates you
3	Does street or hard prescription drugs	Addiction priority over you
4	Drinks to get drunk	Addiction priority over you
5	Smokes or gambles	Addiction priority over you
6	Yells or raises his hand at you	Liable to hit you
7	Hits you	Liable to kill you
8	Wants relationship break	Does not want you Does not respect you
9	Admits he is dating other women	Does not want you
10	Cheats on you	Does not want you or her Does not respect you or her

11	Cheats with you	Does not want you or her Does not respect you or her
12	Watches porn	Will eventually cheat on you Addiction priority over you
13	Wants to be friends with benefits	Does not want you Does not respect you
14	Says he's not ready for marriage	Does not want to marry you
15	Does not love the Lord	Jeopardizing your salvation if you love the Lord

33

Married to the Lord

Turn, O backsliding children, saith the LORD; for I am married unto you: and I will take you one of a city, and two of a family, and I will bring you to Zion: And I will give you pastors according to mine heart, which shall feed you with knowledge and understanding. (Jeremiah 3:14-15)

Once the devil's concubine, now I am married to the Lord. My name is Dawn, I'm a Black woman, and I love Jesus. I used to do licentious[9] things, but I repented and now work for my Lord and Savior, Jesus Christ. I have no wants. I have no needs even though I live in the most expensive city. Once a college dropout turned bachelor's degree holder with a successful career in IT. I will never go hungry when I have the Word of God feeding me. God did not save my soul to keep my story a secret. He wants me to share my testimony with hopes of filling you with the Holy Spirit.

---

[9] Licentious is to indulge excessively in immoral activities with little restraint.

Made in the USA
Middletown, DE
10 September 2021

47962674R00076